D0149057

POEMS OF THE VIKINGS

5.50N

POEMS OF THE VIKINGS

The Elder Edda

Translated by Patricia Terry
with an Introduction by Charles W. Dunn

THE BOBBS-MERRILL COMPANY, INC.
Indianapolis and New York

© 1969 by The Bobbs-Merrill Company, Inc.

Printed in the United States of America

Library of Congress Catalog Card Number 69-16528

ISBN 0-672-60332-2 (pbk)
ISBN 0-672-51052-9

Second Printing

Designed by Blackstarr

FOR KATHARINE AND HENRY WELLS

who have Viking hearts

PREFACE

The Viking poets represented in this book are unimaginable. Beside them Homer appears, if not a precisely outlined figure, at least a known quantity: whoever he may have been, his subjects and his own relationship to his poems seem familiar. The *Edda* poems are extremely varied in content and mood; but tragic or farcical, cosmic or intimate, they all have a strangeness about them, and their particular quality is not to be found anywhere else. This translation was made in the hope that the distinction of these poems could be preserved in a language less forceful than their own, and in a landscape of civilization which is totally different, although its climate might be said to resemble theirs at certain points. But the more the poems impress us as extraordinary, the further, in a sense, we must be from their makers, whose attitudes and perspectives were natural, if not commonplace. Some analysis of these may define what it is that separates us, insofar as this can be stated directly.

Travelers in the Norwegian fjords may have spent hours drifting through clouds of mist interrupted every so often by part of a cliff, straight overhead and immeasurably high, or a white waterfall coming from nowhere. The *Edda* poems, considered as a whole, seem not so much a book as such a panorama, without visible limits in any direction, and containing sharply drawn elements in isolation from one another. One may think first of Valhalla, where gods and men are united in their preparation for the last battle which alone, because they are doomed in advance, can be the perfect occasion for their heroism. Even the world beyond that ultimate destruction can be glimpsed, as when sunlight strikes green grass through the clouds.

Gods and men are both perishable. They are judged by the same general criteria, the men rather more harshly. The virtues of a hero are courage, strength, and loyalty. Elsewhere in the poems ordinary men are praised for prudence, which is often synonymous with wisdom. The gods, unlike the heroes, may be made to look ridiculous—particularly Thor, that personification of strength without intellect who horrifies giants by his gluttony, is teased by the slightly wittier Odin, and is never allowed to forget how he once cowered in the thumb of a glove. All-Father, Odin himself, is dependent on men to the extent that he sometimes allows the weaker of two opponents to win a battle so that the better warrior will be available for Valhalla. The gods are not omniscient; in order to see into the future, Odin must raise witches from the misty lands of Hel. He may acquire knowledge in this way, but he has no more power than men have to change the course of events determined by the Norns. Yet the gods impress us; they are drawn on a larger scale than even the greatest among men, and when they go fishing they catch a World-Serpent, never an eel.

For the most part women and warriors are praised for identical qualities. The poets seem to have been particularly interested in the heroines, perhaps because they may be, like Brynhild, both convincing victims and daughters of Odin. Gudrun herself, the most womanly and the most violent, was a shield-maid according to at least one account of her life. When the warrior husband goes off to fight, however, his valkyrie wife remains at home, a point specifically mentioned in *The Lay of Helgi Hjorvard's Son.* Volund and his brother, on the other hand, enjoy their wives for only seven years; the valkyries cannot be deprived of adventures longer than that. Recognition of maternal sentiments occurs most strikingly in the later poems, sometimes called "Viking Baroque," which relate the horrendous stories of Atli. Here the extreme limit of the praiseworthy desire for revenge is achieved when Gudrun kills her sons. According to *The Lay of Hamdir*'s rather surprising comment, this event hurt Gudrun more than it did Atli.

One imagines that the wives of the Vikings were in fact more "bear-hearted" than it is usual for women to be now, and that the poets wanted to retell the imperfectly remembered Germanic stories at least in part for the pleasure of fashioning the heroines in accordance with their own hearts' desires. Various motives, after all, inspire the warriors, but Brynhild and Gudrun care only for Sigurd, Sigrun for Helgi. It should also be noted that the poems sometimes show Norse men, again unlike the gods, to be very gentle with their wives.

Even *The Waking of Angantyr* may have been intended primarily as the portrait of a woman-warrior, impersonal in her passion for vengeance and courageous enough to acquire and use a sword which is accursed. For us, however, the poem is one of the most compelling because it draws us into that forbidden region "between the worlds" where Hervor talks to her father in his burial mound. Angantyr's body and his spirit are intact in the grave—dissolution seems to be the fate of cowards, and Hervor in her rage wishes it on the invisible warriors—but something in the tone of his voice, weary and even, suggests an infinite distance between him and the girl. Hervor herself, once she has the sword, hurries away from the place where she has walked through the fires of illusion with which the dead frighten the living.

Death, rather than love, is the dominant subject of the *Elder Edda,* but the two may combine in a manner far more satisfying than elsewhere in European poetry because the distinction between the living and the dead is so much vaguer. One of the most beautiful passages describes the meeting of Helgi and Sigrun in the grave. He says that her tears of sorrow fall each night like cold rain onto his shroud. They sleep in each other's arms, but Helgi goes back to Valhalla before dawn and does not return again.

These poems, whether narrative, didactic, or dramatic dialogues, all tend to be lyrical. They are written in stanzas, and show, as W. P. Ker has pointed out, a genius for synthesis which occasionally obscures their stories because the poets have no patience with the dull stretches between climaxes. An Icelandic reader of this translation would be able to distinguish between *fornyrdislag* (the usual meter for narrative poems) and *ljodahattr* ("song" meter), but I can make no claim to metrical accuracy beyond that. I have tried to suggest, if not reproduce, the alliteration. In all other respects, it has been possible to remain very close to the Norse text. The stylistic effects of this poetry, as opposed to those of the more modern court verse, are not so different from English tradition as to impede communication. The Norse is often laconic, sometimes says things obliquely where

English would be direct, and uses a certain number of the kennings—more or less metaphorical synonyms—which became so obtrusive later on. These I have left wherever the context or the reader's experience would explain them, or where they were interesting enough to justify a footnote. Apart from such embellishments, the language of the *Edda* is simple and free from archaisms; I have tried to keep mine the same.

The translations follow Gustav Neckel's 1962 edition, except for departures indicated in the notes; the majority of these were suggested by R. C. Boer in his edition of the *Edda.* Two poems, *The Lay of Rig* and *The Song of Hyndla,* inferior in quality and preservation, have been omitted, as well as those sections of the *Codex Regius* which are entirely in prose, and occasional passages from other poems as noted.

Four people have been indispensable to this work: Professor Charles Donahue of Fordham University, who suggested it and so generously gave me lessons in Old Norse; Professor Charles Dunn, whose critical reading meant peace of mind for the translator; Starr Atkinson, most sensitive of editors; and my husband, who has been willing to share his home with so many Vikings for so long.

Patricia Terry

CONTENTS

xi

Deyr fé, deyia fraendr,
  deyr siálfr it sama;
en orztírr deyr aldregi,
  hveim er sér góðan getr.

Cattle die, kinsmen die,
  one day you die yourself;
but the words of praise will not perish
  when a man wins fair fame.

(*Sayings of the High One*, 76)

The poems that are here so vividly translated by Patricia Terry unfold the traditional lore of the Norsemen concerning their gods and heroes. "Fair fame" is their chief subject; and such has been the potency of their "words of praise" that Odin the god, Sigurd the hero, and Brynhild the valkyrie still live. But who were the poets? Ironically, all we know of them is that they were the kinsmen of the Viking warriors who are popularly thought of as savage pirates of the western seas. Their literary legacy therefore deserves careful assessment.

In the remote obscurity of the past the adventurous Germanic ancestors of the Norsemen had carried their culture and their particular Germanic dialects from the mainland of Europe northward first into Denmark, Sweden, and Norway, then by the year 874 into Iceland, and by A.D. 986 into Greenland. Thereafter, as skilled seamen they set no limits to their explorations. From their Scandinavian bases they established beachheads at almost every estuary in western Europe. They founded notable realms in Normandy and in the English Danelaw. They sailed through the Mediterranean and settled in Sicily; they passed over the Black Sea; they penetrated the Baltic and settled in what is now Russia; they sailed around the North Cape to the isolated White Sea; and they traveled at large across the wide Atlantic. They supported their travels by ransacking (this was one of their own Norse words borrowed into English); but presumably they considered their activities to be expansive rather than aggressive. As Caesar said of their continental forefathers, "those raids which they make beyond the boundaries of each community are not in any way considered disgraceful."

The Scandinavians were, indeed, much more than raiders. They brought law (another Norse word); they established trade; and they carried a rich oral culture. They tenaciously retained their native mythology, religion, beliefs, rites, and cults until at last in approximately the year 1000, after much deliberation, they adopted Christianity.

The lays here translated are basically a product of the pre-Christian Norse culture of Norway and Iceland. For the most part they are survivals typical of the oral culture of the tenth century, but we know them only as they were written down by antiquarian Christian scribes in the thirteenth century. The great Icelandic historian Snorri Sturluson (who died in 1241) led the way in recording his native traditions by compiling a handbook of pre-Christian Norse lore known as *The Prose Edda* (or, misleadingly, *The Younger Edda*). Following his lead, anonymous compilers recorded the fragments of their ancient poetic tradition. Their collection of poems known as *The Elder Edda,* upon which we are principally dependent for our knowledge of this vanishing repertoire, provides a priceless but incomplete and partial sampling of the great period of Old Norse poetry.

The oldest extant manuscript of *The Elder Edda,* the *Codex Regius,* was compiled in Iceland at a date no earlier than 1270. The poems which it contains vary in antiquity and are marred by gaps and discrepancies.

The pre-Christian composers and singers who had circulated the poems obviously served as custodians of the pagan lore cherished by their people. The later scribes, on the contrary, neither accepted nor wholly understood the old religious myths; they did not entirely believe in the historicity of the ancient legends; and the wisdom cherished in the poetry of the Heroic Age had lost much of its relevance for a people whose prosperity depended no longer upon war-galleys and swords but upon farms and merchant ships. The marvel is that so much has survived of their lore concerning the gods and heroes and so much of their poetic wisdom.

The Gods

Þá gengo regin ǫll   á rǫkstóla,
ginnheilog goð,   ok um þat gaettoz.

Then all the gods   met to give judgment,
the holy gods   took counsel together.

(*The Sibyl's Prophecy*, 6)

It is difficult now to reconstruct Norse religion—as difficult, in fact, as if a latter-day archaeologist were forced to reconstruct Christianity from an excavation that yielded only a fourteenth-century crucifix, a piece of Victorian stained glass, and a twentieth-century Christmas-tree light. As in most primitive religions, the Norse concept was comprehensive and systematic; the relation of the gods to man provided a vital working hypothesis concerning the origin and nature of man's universe. The function of the myths, as of Kipling's *Just So Stories,* was in part etiological. At the same time, as in most primitive religions, the pre-Christian Norse believed that, by sacrifices and other cult practices, they could avert misfortune and propitiate the gods and obtain their assistance. Thus the function of the gods might be said also to be providential, though one must add that the gods seem to have been poor providers.

The common Germanic system was complex and subject to many inconsistencies and local variations. The Norse gods differed in kind (the Aesir and the Vanir), and they were opposed by various sorts of demons known as giants and dwarves. They were, moreover, subject to fate even as men are. Over them forever hung the impending doom known as "the fate of the gods" or, in Wagner's famous mistranslation, "the twilight of the gods."

The leading gods clearly played varied roles. Odin, for instance, the father of all, was the director of battle. He commanded the valkyries, who (as the etymology of the name suggests) "chose out" those who were to be slain in combat. In order to gain victory, Norse warriors used to sacrifice their prisoners to him, and they hoped that they could spend their own afterlife in his Valhalla, where their bravery would be rewarded by eternal banqueting and fighting. As the one-eyed seer, however, Odin was also the god of knowledge who knew the past, the present, and the future.

Odin's son Thor, the god of thunder, controlled the forces of nature, and as the supreme wielder of weapons he was therefore revered by hard-smiting warriors. It is no coincidence that his name appears as the first element in innumerable Norse personal names such as Thorberg, Thorbrand, Thorfinn, Thorgrim, Thorkell, Thorsteinn, Thorvald, and the like; such names were doubtless given by parents anxious to obtain Thor's protection for'their sons.

Among the Vanir, on the other hand, Frey and Freyja, the brother-and-sister divinities, controlled fertility. In *The Lay of Thrym* the poet does not treat Freyja very seriously, but her role must once have been considered most important. Not only did she and her brother control the propagation of all living things; they could also provide continuity to a family line by effecting the rebirth of a hero or heroine. Before the adoption of Christianity their favors were desperately courted in fertility rites which later converts have hesitated to describe in detail.

The impact of Christianity upon Norse belief was obviously shattering. During Saint Olaf's mission in Norway (*ca.* 1021), for instance, Gudbrand of Loar tried to turn back the Christians by producing the portable shrine of Thor. Thanks to a miracle carefully prearranged by Saint Olaf, the idol burst apart, and from it "mice as big as cats, adders, and serpents" sprang forth. Disgruntled with his god, Gudbrand became a Christian, remarking opportunistically to Olaf that, since the old god "couldn't help us, we'll now believe in the god in whom you believe."

In somewhat the same spirit, during the conversion of the Icelanders (A.D. 1000), Hjalti composed an impromptu verse:

I don't wish to revile the gods,
but Freyja seems to me a bitch.

But even if Hjalti could no longer approve of the tales and rituals associated with the time-honored goddess of fertility, it seems most unlikely that he was able immediately to forget and abandon all his inherited beliefs.

Naturally the later scribes who recorded *The Poetic Edda* were just as skeptical as Hjalti had been. One of them writes (at the end of *The Second Lay of Helgi Hunding's Bane*) concerning the doctrine of reincarnation: "In olden times it was believed that people could be born again, although that is now considered an old woman's tale." Yet the scribe does not seem to have carried his skepticism far beyond Hjalti's; his care in recording the old belief betrays his respect for a lay which he obviously wishes to preserve.

The Heroes

"Munak ek floeia,   þótt mik feigan viᴢir,
  emka ek meðˇ   bleyðˇi borinn."

"I will not flee   though you foretell my death—
  I was never called a coward."

(*The Lay of Sigrdrifa,* 21)

Like the mythology of the Germanic gods, the legends of the Germanic heroes were not particularly compatible with Christianity. To be sure, the heroic ideals were noble and magnificent. The hero wrestled on behalf of his people with the conflicting forces of love and war and fate. Yet the ethics of Sigurd, or of his German counterpart Siegfried, are not the ethics of Christianity.

The heroes are, moreover, legendary rather than historical; and their actions are significantly controlled by the supernatural forces that were an accepted part of the Norse mythological system. The purely historical basis of the whole cycle of lays connected with Sigurd can, in fact, be summarized within the brief compass of a single diagram:

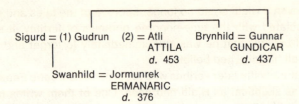

Gunnar (Gudrun's brother) corresponds to the historical Gundicar, king of the Germanic tribe of Burgundians who were defeated and displaced in 437 by the invading Huns. Atli (Gudrun's second husband) corresponds to the notorious Attila, king of the Huns, who overran much of northern Europe. Jormunrek corresponds to Ermanaric, king of the once-powerful Goths, who has here, with considerable chronological violence, been dragged into the story of Sigurd.

The other characters in the cycle do not even have any historical prototypes. All the related Germanic legends agree that Sigurd is the son of Sigmund; but Sigmund the son of Volsung, who claims direct descent from Odin, is partly legendary and partly mythological. Brynhild, the *femme fatale* of the Sigurd cycle, was one of Odin's valkyries and was obviously thought of, in the pre-Christian tradition, as a supernatural being.

The tribal history involved in the tale of Sigurd is just as obscure to the singers of the Norse lays as the individual identity of the heroes. Sigurd's father, we are told, is king of the Franks —a plausible enough identification, since the powerful Germanic tribe of Franks did in fact continue to hold their territory at the mouth of the Rhine even when Attila drove the neighboring Burgundians south and extended his empire to the eastern banks of the Rhine. Sigurd himself, however, is inconsistently referred to as king of the Huns; and Gunnar, the king of the Burgundians, is sometimes quite impossibly referred to as king of the Goths. And the vaguely imagined territory of Atli, though it is consistently enough referred to as Hunland, seems a shadowy thing compared to that vast historical empire of Attila so vividly described by Gibbon in *The Decline and Fall of the Roman Empire.*

For the singers who composed the heroic lays five hundred years or more after the event, these tribal divisions understandably had little significance. What concerned them was the heroic ideal of an imagined past. Essentially, the *leitmotif* of all their songs, though variously developed by the singers, was the human dilemma of divided loyalties. They well understood that the demands of familial duty to one's kinsmen and of martial allegiance to one's lord were inexorable. They knew, too, that duty and allegiance constantly required the hero to defend his honor and to execute revenge. Within this rigid Germanic tribal system they realized that human affection, friendship, and love could play only a poignantly helpless role. Such matters are the very sum and substance of the heroic lays, just as they are of the later Norse sagas and, significantly, of the last great reworking of Scandinavian legend in European literature, namely Shakespeare's *Hamlet*.

The pessimistic determinism of the heroic lays seems also to reflect the fundamental assumptions of Norse mythology. The myths could provide an explanation for the origin of evil, but they could supply no cure. If Ibsen had written the tale of Sigurd, he would no doubt have emphasized the human fact that the hero was destroyed by an over-ambitious mother-in-law. The Norse poets, however, imply that Sigurd and all his friends and foes were doomed to destruction because of the gods. The immediate enemy of the people is Regin the dwarf, whom the poet aptly calls "the folk-destroying enemy." It is through him that Sigurd wins for mankind the supernatural treasure, and the treasure bears a curse upon it. The ultimate cause of the curse, in turn, is the crime of Loki, the laughing, mischievous, indifferent, sinister giant. His capricious slaying of Otter the dwarf precipitates a long chain of obligatory acts of vengeance in which gods, giants, dwarves, and human beings all suffer.

Summarized in bare narrative form, the tribal warfare of the Franks, Burgundians, and Huns may seem not to differ much from present-day gangland slayings, but the singers of the lays saw a cosmic meaning in their songs. Heroes and heroines do what they must, and their fate in this unfriendly universe can at least be explained by a supernatural cause even if it cannot be justified.

Wisdom

Heill, sá er kvað!   Heill, sá er kann!
  Nióti, sá er nam!
  Heilir, þeirs hlýddo!

Hail to the speaker!   Hail the one he taught!
  They're lucky who have the lore,
  happy if they heed it.

(*Sayings of the High One,* 164)

The all-wise god Odin gave his eye in order to acquire wisdom; and Sigurd, in his wooing of Brynhild, spent most of his time in absorbing her supernaturally acquired lore. Like the gods and the heroes, the Norse singers of lays also treasured wisdom for wisdom's sake. To modern readers of the lays, the poet's preoccupation with sententiousness may seem both irrelevant and unaesthetic, but the role of the pre-Christian Norse poet was that of a shaman, a tribal seer. He was not primarily concerned, like a romantic poet, with the creation of beauty; rather he was expected, through his control of the magical process of poetry, to discover and reveal wisdom. The poet was not only obliged to narrate the deeds of the gods and heroes; he was also required to prescribe pungently and memorably in his gnomic verse the kind of behavior appropriate to heroes. If his sententious utterances sometimes sound a trifle fatuous, the same may often be said of well-intentioned advice including that contained in medieval courtesy books or modern guides to etiquette. And usually, it must be admitted, his sententious utterances are dramatically appropriate and manifestly true.

There is only one particular form of poetic wisdom that demands special judgment, and that is the encyclopedic listing of esoteric mythological details such as are itemized in *The Lay of Grimnir.* The key to this treasure-trove has been lost. Yet even here the reader, like a sympathetic anthropologist on his first visit to some strange tribal ceremony, can reach some appreciation for the poetry if he remembers that the Norsemen once considered such lore to be vital to their well-being.

Style

As Patricia Terry's flexible translations suggest, the style of the lays varies greatly. Some early lays are written in standard meters; others contain loose, eccentric stanzas; and some of the late accretions to *The Edda* tend towards a complex and decorative style. Scholars have traditionally scanned the lays by a system devised in the nineteenth century by Eduard Sievers, but the relevance of his rigorous doctrine to actual compositional techniques now seems questionable. Suffice it to say that the reciter (who possibly sang to a musical accompaniment) composed his lines, like most oral performers, on the basis of customary formulas and tied them together in stanzaic units.

Typically the stanza contains four lines; each line is divided by a caesura; and each line is decorated by an alliteration connecting a stressed initial sound in the first half to a stressed initial sound in the second half of the line. (Any vowel alliterates with itself or any other vowel.) Each half-line contains two stresses unrestricted as to position. The archaic stanza known as *fornyrdislag* or "ancient verse" allows generally only two unstressed syllables per half-line; another similar stanza, known as *málaháttr* or "speech verse," allows three unstressed syllables per half-line. Typical is the following:

Veit ek á fialli   fólk-vitr sofa,
ok leikr yfir   lindar-váði.
Yggr stakk þorni;   aðra feldi,
hǫrgefn, hali,   en hafa vildi.

(Literally: I know on the fell a folk-
protectress sleeps, and there licks above

her the linden's foe [fire]. The frightful
one [Odin] stuck a thorn in her; other men
she had felled, the linen-giver [lady], other
than he had wished to have.)

(*The Lay of Fafnir*, 43)

A different stanza, known as the *ljódaháttr*, "song-measure,"
contains first and third lines like those just described, alternating
with three-stressed second and fourth lines:

Þagalt ok hugalt   skyli þióðans barn
 ok víg-diarft vera.
Glaðr ok reifr   skyli gumna hverr,
 unz sinn bíðr bana.

(Silent and thoughtful ought a king's son
to be and battle-bold. Contented and
cheerful ought every man to be till in
time he meets death.)

(*Sayings of the High One*, 15)

The reader can best realize the effect of such poetry by re-
citing it aloud either in the original or in Patricia Terry's translation, which imitates the effects of the original. The melody, it
will be noticed, arises not just from the alliterative echoes, but
from the contrast of alliterating and non-alliterating stressed
sounds. Diagrammatically, the two stanzas quoted above present the following patterns:

(1) V F – F S   (2) TH H – TH B
  L Y – L V   V D V
  Y TH – A F   G R – G H
  H H – H V   S B B

The ear is constantly affected by the unpredictable alternations of similarities and dissimilarities; and, because of the freedom of the syllabic count, the placement of the beat in each half-line is also unpredictably varied. One can train oneself to hear such music; and music it is.

The literal translations accompanying the preceding metrical illustrations serve at the same time to suggest two further characteristics of the lays, namely, the tight interweaving of the words within each stanza and the rich allusiveness of their language. But the most subtle consideration in our reading of the lays is less a question of technique than of tone. The scribes may have lost their faith, but the poets who preceded them treated their subject matter with a high seriousness. The poet's attitude towards the gods may seem frivolous in *The Lay of Thrym,* but if so the frivolousness is of a nervous kind. More typically, as in *The Sibyl's Prophecy,* the gods are viewed as awesome, remote, and mysterious beings. Man's life is thought of as essentially tragic; an inexorable fate constantly threatens to snatch him away to a cold and cheerless after-world.

The deepest kind of human passion lies implicit in the narratives, but the stern poets of the Heroic Age seldom choose to give it expression. Oddrun may for a moment sound like a Victorian heroine when, in describing her love affair with Gunnar, she says, "We were not strong enough to strive with love." But her utterance was not intended romantically. The more typical expression of love is to be found rather in *The Short Lay of Sigurd* at that terrible and tragic moment when the vengeful Brynhild laughs speechlessly after discovering that the only man in the world whom she could love has been killed.

The intensity of this heroic tone is, of course, not always maintained; and the late *Greenland Lay of Atli,* in particular, descends from the noble to the most utterly banal. But in general the Norse lays represent a high achievement in the literary history of Europe. On later readers they have exercised various kinds of fascinations. From a lay in *The Elder Edda* and another embedded in *Njal's Saga,* Thomas Gray in the eighteenth century distilled the essence of Gothic horror. A century later Richard

Wagner converted the legend of a hero and valkyrie into a drama of high romantic passion. In the twentieth century the student can read the lays in the light of the solid results achieved by intensive and detached scholarship; he can understand them historically and appraise them comparatively. But, best of all, through translation everyone can admire the sparkling brilliance of their iceberg-like beauty.

Charles W. Dunn
Harvard University

SELECTED WORKS OF REFERENCE

Bibliography

Hermannsson, Halldór. *Bibliography of the Eddas* (Islandica 13). Ithaca: Cornell University Press, 1931.

Hannesson, Johann S. *Supplement to Bibliography of the Eddas* (Islandica 37). Ithaca: Cornell University Press, 1955.

Editions

Boer, R. C., ed. *Die Edda.* 2 vols. Haarlem, 1922.

Neckel, Gustav, ed. *Die Lieder des Codex Regius.* Vol. I: 2nd edition, ed. H. Kuhn, Heidelberg, 1962. Vol. II, 1927.

Sijmons, B., and Hugo Gering, eds. *Die Lieder der Edda.* 3 vols. in 4. Halle, 1888-1931.

Literary History

Ellis Davidson, H. R. *Gods and Myths of Northern Europe.* Harmondsworth: Penguin, 1964.

Einarsson, Stefán. *A History of Icelandic Literature.* New York: Johns Hopkins, 1957.

Ker, W. P. *Epic and Romance.* New York: Dover Publications, 1957.

————. The Dark Ages. New York: New American Library, 1958.

Philpotts, Bertha S. *The Elder Edda.* Cambridge, 1920.

Turville-Petre, E. O. G. *Myth and Religion of the North.* New York: Holt, Rinehart & Winston, 1964.

————. *Origins of Icelandic Literature.* Oxford: Oxford University Press, 1953.

de Vries, Jan. *Heroic Song and Heroic Legend.* Trans. B. J. Timmer. London, 1963

Young, Jean I., trans. *The Prose Edda*. Cambridge, 1955; Berkeley, 1966.

Dictionaries

Zoëga, Geir T. *A Concise Dictionary of Old Icelandic*. Oxford, 1961.

Vigfusson, Gudbrand. *An Icelandic-English Dictionary*. Oxford, 1874.

POEMS OF THE VIKINGS

THE SIBYL'S PROPHECY

A prophetess speaks to Odin about the world's creation and the doom of the gods.

Grant me silence,   you holy gods
and all men everywhere,   Heimdal's sons,
while Warfather listens   to the ancient lore,
the oldest runes   that I remember.

I know giants   of ages past,
those who called me   one of their kin;
I know how nine roots   form nine worlds
below the Earth   where the Ash Tree rises.

When Ymir lived,   long ages ago,
before there were seas,   chill waves or shore,
Earth was not yet   nor the high heavens
but a great emptiness   nowhere green.

Then Bur's sons   lifted up the land
and made Midgard   for men to dwell in;
the sun shone   out of the south,
and bright grass grew   from the ground of stone.

The sun climbed;   the moon's companion
raised its right hand   over heaven's rim.
The sun did not know   where its hall would stand,
the stars did not know   where they would be set,
the moon did not know   what would be its might.

Warfather. Odin, "the father of the slain," who has asked the sibyl to tell him the fate of the gods.

Bur's sons. Giants.

Midgard. The earth, a circular zone in the center of a flat disc. It is located beneath Asgard, the home of the gods, and is surrounded by a sea, beyond which is Utgard or Jotunheim, the home of giants. Below Midgard is Niflheim, "Mist-Home," the kingdom of Hel, Loki's daughter, who rules the dead.

1–5

Then all the gods   met to give judgment,
the holy gods   took counsel together:
they named night   and the waning moon,
they gave names   to morning and midday,
afternoon and evening,   ordered time by years.

The Aesir met   in Idavelli;
they built altars,   high timbered halls,
fashioned hearths   to forge gold treasure,
strong tools   and heavy tongs.

Cheerful, they sat   over games of chess—
they never knew   any lack of gold—
until three Norns came,   loathsome to look at,
giant maidens   from Jotunheim.

And of the Aesir   assembled there
three of the holy ones   left the hall;
they found on land   two feeble trees,
the Ash and the Elm,   with no fixed fate.

These did not breathe,   nor had they feeling,
speech or craft,   bearing, color;
Odin gave life's breath,   Hoenir gave feeling,
Lodur gave craft,   bearing, color.

There is an ash tree—   its name is Yggdrasil—
a tall tree sparkling   with clear drops of dew
which fall from its boughs   down into the valleys;
ever green it stands   beside the Norns' spring.

There live three maidens   wise in lore
in a hall which stands   beneath that tree:

. . . from Jotunheim. The next stanzas, 9 through 16, contain a catalogue of
dwarf names. They have not been included.
. . . and the Elm. The identification of this second tree is uncertain.
Hoenir gave feeling. According to Vigfusson, speech was part of Hoenir's gift.

one is Urd,   another is Verdandi,
—they have carved out runes—   Skuld is the third;
they established laws,   decided the lives
men were to lead,   marked out their fates.

URD · PAST
VERDANDI · PRESENT
SKULD · FUTURE

I remember war,   the first in the world:
the Aesir struck   Gullveig with spears
and burned her body   in Har's hall;
three times burned,   three times born,
again and again,   yet she is still alive.

She was called Heid   in the halls that knew her,
a sibyl skilled   at looking into time;
she used magic   to ensnare the mind,
a welcome friend   to wicked women.

Then the mighty gods   met to give judgment,
the holy gods   took counsel together:
would the Vanir claim   victory tribute,
or with the Aesir   unite in peace?

Odin took aim   and shot into the host—
that was the first war   in the world.
The wall of Asgard   crashed to the ground;
the Vanir marched   to meet their foes.

Then the mighty gods   met to give judgment,
the holy gods   took counsel together:
who had let evil   into the world,
and offered to giants   Od's wife, Freyja?

Thor alone, raging,   got revenge—
he didn't often   take insults lying down;

I remember war. Here, as elsewhere in the poem, the sibyl is referred to in the third person. The identification of Gullveig is uncertain.

or with the Aesir. Hostages were eventually exchanged, among them Frey, Freyja, and Njord, their father. Then the Aesir and the Vanir ruled together.

vows were broken,   promises and oaths,
the solemn treaties   both sides had sworn.

I can say where Heimdal's   horn is hidden:
beneath the holy tree   which hides the sun;
a waterfall keeps   the branches cool—
it flows from Odin's eye.   Seek you wisdom still?

I sat outside alone;   the old one came,
the lord of the Aesir,   and looked into my face:
"Why have you come here?   What would you ask me?
I know, Odin,   how you lost your eye:
it lies in the water   of Mimir's well."
Every morning   Mimir drinks mead
from Warfather's tribute.   Seek you wisdom still?

Odin gave me   gold and treasure;
I looked far   into the future,
spoke with wisdom   of all the worlds.

I saw valkyries—   they came from everywhere,
ready to ride   to the lands of men;
Skuld held a shield,   so did Skogul,
Gunn was there, Held,   Gondul, Geirskogul.
Now you know   the names of the shield-maids
sent by Odin   to the slain.

I saw Balder   stained with blood,
I saw the fate   of Odin's son:
above the fields,   fragile and fair,
climbed the slender   mistletoe.

---

it flows from Odin's eye. That is, from Mimir's well. Mimir is a giant, keeper of
the Well of Wisdom under a root of Yggdrasil. Odin sacrificed his eye in return
for a drink at the well.

mead/from Warfather's tribute. The "mead" is the magical water from Mimir's
well.

From that same plant   which seemed so frail
Hod selected   his fatal shaft;
Balder's brother   was born soon after,
and one night old   avenged Odin's son.

He would not wash his hands   or comb his hair
till Balder's foe   burned on the pyre;
but Frigg wept   in Fensalir
for Valhall's sorrow.   Seek you wisdom still?

I saw in chains   under the kettle-wood
someone who looked   like guileful Loki;
there sits Sigyn—   she doesn't seem
happy for her husband.   Seek you wisdom still?

A river bears eastward   through a baneful valley
swords and spears;   it's called the Slid.

There stood to the north   at Nidafells
a golden hall,   the home of dwarfs;
there was another   at Okalnir,
a giant's beer-hall;   Brimir is his name.

Far from sunlight   stood a hall
on the Shores of the Dead;   its doors faced north.
Deadly poisons   dripped through its roof,
the rooms writhed   with twisting snakes.

I saw men wading   through heavy streams:
some were oath-breakers,   others had murdered,

From that same plant. Loki knew that only the mistletoe, of all living things,
had not sworn to protect Balder; thus Loki caused blind Hod to kill his brother.
Balder was avenged by Vali, who was born to Odin and the giantess Rind.

for Valhall's sorrow. Following stanza 33, Neckel includes two lines which are
omitted here, as they are in Boer's edition.

under the kettle-wood. This seems to mean a wood with hot springs, which
points to the landscape of Iceland. The eruptions of geysers are said to be
caused by Loki's struggles to escape (Boer).

some had lured   another man's love.
There the Serpent   sucked on corpses,
the Wolf rent dead men.   Seek you wisdom still?

Eastward, the old one   in the Iron Wood
raises the wolves   of Fenrir's race;
one is destined   to be some day
the monstrous beast   who destroys the moon.

He sucks out   the strength of the dying,
colors the heavens   crimson with their blood;
there will be dark sunshine   the summer after,
and evil weather.   Seek you wisdom still?

He sat on a grave-mound,   striking a harp,
Eggther, glad   to guard the giants;
close to him   the bright red cock,
Fjalar, crowed   in the Forest of Birds.

And in Asgard   Gold-Comb crowed,
the cock who wakes   Odin's warriors;
another is heard   below the Earth,
a soot-red cock   in the halls of Hel.

Garm bays loudly   from Gnipa Cave;
his rope will break   and he will run free.
Many spells I know,   and I can see
the doom that awaits   the almighty gods.

---

the old one. Presumably their mother, the goddess Angrbotha.

He sat on a grave-mound. The first two lines of this stanza are interpreted according to Boer.

Gold-Comb, or Gullinkambi, awakens the warriors in Valhalla to each day's combat, after which those who have been killed are restored to life. These battles are fought in preparation for the last—the Ragnarok, or Doom of the Gods—which they are doomed to lose. Here the cocks crow at the beginning of this final conflict.

Brothers will die,   slain by their brothers,
incest will break   kinship's bonds;
woe to the world then,   wedded to whoredom,
battle-axe and sword rule,   split shields asunder,
storm-cleft age of wolves   until the world goes down,
only hatred   in the hearts of men.

Mim's sons play;   now fate will summon
from its long sleep   the Gjallarhorn:
Heimdal's horn   clamors to heaven,
dead Mim's head speaks   tidings to Odin.

Lofty Yggdrasil,   the Ash Tree, trembles,
ancient wood groaning;   the giant goes free.

How fare the Aesir?   How do the Elves fare?
Jotunheim groans,   the gods meet in council,
at the stone doorways   of deep stone dwellings
dwarfs are moaning.   Seek you wisdom still?

Garm bays loudly   from Gnipa Cave,
his rope will break,   and he will run free.

Westward drives the giant,   Hrym, his shield high;
the world-girding Serpent   rises from the water,
lashing at the waves;   the bright-beaked eagle
rends corpses, screaming;   Naglfar sails free.

Southward the ship sails;   ruin by fire,
fiends led by Loki,   flies across the sea,

Gjallarhorn. The horn buried under the Ash tree.

dead Mim's head. Another explanation of Odin's wisdom. With herbs and charms Odin preserved Mimir's head, cut off by the Vanir, and received wise counsel from it.

Lofty Yggdrasil. Neckel adds two more lines here, as in stanza 48.

Southward the ship sails. As in Boer.

monstrous companions   to his wolf brood;
Byleist's brother,   Loki, leads them.

Surt fares northward,   lord of the fire-giants;
his sword of flame   gleams like the sun;
crashing rocks drag   demons to their doom;
men find the way to Hel   as the sky splits open.

The second sorrow   comes to Odin's wife:
Odin goes forth   to fight the Wolf.
Frey, Beli's slayer,   battles with Surt;
thus will Freyja's   loved one fall.

Garm bays loudly   from Gnipa Cave;
his rope will break   and he will run free.

Odin's son Vithar   goes to fight the Wolf;
then in the heart   of the carrion beast,
Loki's foul son,   stands Vithar's sword.
So is the god   Odin avenged.

Far-famed Thor,   the son of Earth,
the son of Odin,   battles with the Snake.
Nine steps beyond   the serpent's fury
Hlodin's son   still walks in pride.

Dark is the sun,   the Earth sinks below the sea,
no bright star now   shines from the heavens;

comes to Odin's wife. Frigg, or Hlin, the goddess of love. Her first sorrow was
Balder's death.

Far-famed Thor. The following lines have been omitted from this stanza:
    He strikes in wrath   Midgard's protector;
    now will all men   leave their homes.
It is uncertain whether "Midgard's protector" (Thor) is nominative or accusative
here, and the following line, although defensible, is unconvincing. Thor killed
the Snake, but died of its venom.

only smoke   and menacing fires
leap to the skies   in lordly flame.

I see rising   a second time
out of the waters   the Earth, green once more;
an eagle flies   over rushing waterfalls,
hunting for fish   from the craggy heights.

The Aesir meet   in Idavelli;
they speak together   about the Serpent,
looking again   at days long past,
remembering Odin's   ancient runes.

In later times   a wondrous treasure,
chessmen of gold,   will be found in the grass
where the Aesir had left them   ages ago.

Barren fields   will bear again,
woes will be cured   when Balder comes:
Hod and Balder   will live in Odin's hall,
home of the war-gods.   Seek you wisdom still?

From bloody twigs   Hoenir tells the future;
the sons of Ve and Vili   dwell in the sky,
home of the wide winds.   Seek you wisdom still?

The mighty one comes down   on the day of doom,
that powerful lord   who rules over all.

I see a hall   fairer than the sun,
thatched with gold;   it stands at Gimli.
There shall deserving   people dwell
to the end of time   and enjoy their happiness.

. . . in lordly flame. Stanza 53 occurs again after this line. It is obviously mis-
placed, and has been deleted here.
the mighty one. This stanza is sometimes considered a reference to Christ.

There comes the dark   dragon flying,
flashing upward   from Nidafells;
on wide swift wings   it soars above the Earth
carrying dead bodies.   Now it will sink down.

Now it will sink down. That is, disappear in the new order. Another interpretation has it that the sibyl sinks down at the end of her prophecy.

SAYINGS OF THE HIGH ONE

The various sections of this poem teach Viking manners and morals; rune lore, including a mystical passage (stanzas 138– 141) in which Odin acquires his wisdom; and the unreliability of women, as illustrated by Odin's adventures. The title refers only to stanzas 111–164; the poem as a whole probably originated in Norway.

At every doorway   what you have to do
   is look around you
   and look out;
never forget: no matter where you are
   you might find a foe.

Hail to hosts!   A guest is in the hall,
   where shall he sit down?
To please him, quickly   give him a place
   in front of the blazing fire.

There must be a fire   for the frozen knees
   of all arriving guests,
food and clothing   for those who come
   over the hills to your hall.

There must be water   when guests come to a meal,
   towels and a welcome to the table;
it's good manners   to give them both
   talk and a turn to speak.

It takes sharp wits   to travel in the world—
   they're not so hard on you at home;
in the flicker of an eye   the fool is found
   who wanders among the wise.

Hail to hosts. "Hosts" is a translation of "givers." The meaning of the last two lines of this stanza is somewhat questionable.

Better to be careful   than to boast
    how much is in your mind;
when the wise come in,   keeping their counsel,
    trouble seldom starts.
A man won't find   a better friend
    than his own head full of sense.

The careful guest   comes to a meal
    and sits in wary silence;
with his eyes and ears   wide open,
    every wise man keeps watch.

Happy is the man   who hears of himself
    well-meant words of praise;
it's hard to know   what may be hidden
    in another man's mind.

Lucky the man   who can look to himself
    to provide his praise and wisdom;
evil counsel   has often come
    out of another man's mind.

If a man takes with him   a mind full of sense
    he can carry nothing better;
riches like this   on a stranger's road
    will do more good than gold.

If a man takes with him   a mind full of sense
    he can carry nothing better;
nothing is worse   to carry on your way
    than a head heavy with beer.

Beer isn't such   a blessing to men
    as it's supposed to be;
the more you swallow,   the less you stay
    the master of your mind.

The mind-stealing heron   hovers over feasts
   waiting to seize men's wits;
that bird's feathers   fettered me
   when I came to Gunnlod's court.

I was drunk,   four sheets to the wind,
   at Fjalar's feast;
from the best carousing   a man will come
   to his senses soon again.

Silent and thoughtful   a king's son should be
   and bold in battle;
merry and glad   every man should be
   until the day he dies.

The foolish man   thinks he'll live forever
   if he stays away from war,
but old age   shows him no mercy
   though the spears spare him.

The stupid man   on a visit stares,
   he mutters or he mopes;
all he has to do   is take a drink
   and what wit he has collapses.

A man must go   to many places,
   travel widely in the world,
before he is wise enough   to see the workings
   of other men's minds.

The mind-stealing heron. This incident occurred during Odin's visit to Suttung, related in stanzas 104ff. Heron feathers may work magic, or may represent a more common mind-stealer at feasts. At Suttung's court, Odin was certainly in possession of his senses, apparently after losing them. Fjalar is presumably Suttung.

and what wit he has collapses. The conclusion of this stanza has been somewhat differently interpreted; Cleasby-Vigfusson gives "what wit he has awakens," that is, his spirits rise. Or the line may mean that one can see the quality of a fool's wits when he takes a drink.

Don't cling to the cup   but drink your share,
   speak useful words or be silent;
no one will blame you   for bad manners
   if you go to bed early.

A greedy man   if he lets himself go
   will eat until he's ill;
when such a one   sits with the wise,
   they mock the stupidity of stomachs.

The herds know   when it's time to go home
   and give up grazing,
but a foolish man   will always forget
   the size of his stomach.

An evil-tempered,   small-minded man
   is scornful of what he sees;
he alone   is unaware
   that he's not free from faults.

A stupid man   stays awake all night
   pondering his problems;
he's worn out   when morning comes
   and whatever was, still is.

The foolish man   thinks everyone his friend
   who laughs when he does;
if wise men mock him   behind his back,
   he'll never know.

The foolish man   thinks everyone his friend
   who laughs when he does;
then he sees   that few will take his side
   when his case comes to court.

When the stupid man   sits in his corner,
   there's nothing he doesn't know;

he'll find that difficult   to demonstrate
   if someone tries him out.

When a stupid man   comes into company
   he'd better be silent;
no one will notice   that he knows nothing
   unless he talks a lot.
(And if he talks   to men of like talent
   it's safe for him to speak.)

A clever man   will ask questions
   and answer as well;
no one can hope   to keep anything concealed
   once it is heard in a hall.

A man who speaks   and is never silent
   is bound to blunder;
a ready tongue,   if it's not restrained,
   will do you damage.

Take more than a moment   to judge a man
   who comes on a visit;
many seem clever   if they're asked no questions
   and don't stay out in storms.

A man is wise   to be far away
   when one guest goads another;
he may sit at the table   in friendly talk
   and then learn he laughed with foes.

Even friends   fond of each other
   will fight at table;
nothing will ever   bring to an end
   the strife of men at meals.

(And if he talks . . .). Parentheses mine. The translation here assumes that *madr*
refers to the listener, *hann* in the next line to the foolish speaker.

A man does well   to eat a hearty meal
  before he visits friends,
or he sits around glumly   acting starved
  and finds words for very few.

A bad friend   lives far away
  though his house lie on your road,
but it's no distance   to one who is dear
  though you travel many miles.

Don't stay forever   when you visit friends,
  know when it's time to leave;
love turns to loathing   if you sit too long
  on someone else's bench.

Though it be little,   better to live
  in a house you hold as your own;
with just two goats,   and ropes for rafters,
  you're better off than begging.

Though it be little,   better to live
  in a house you hold as your own;
a man's heart breaks   if he has to beg
  for everything he eats.

Don't leave your weapons   lying about
  behind your back in a field;
you never know   when you may need
  all of a sudden your spear.

I've never met   a man so generous
  you couldn't give him a gift,
nor one so pleased   to part with his property
  he didn't care what cash came in.

A man should spend   his hard-earned money
  on whatever he may want;

saving for dear ones   may serve the detested:
    things often don't work out our way.

Give your friends gifts—   they're as glad as you are
    to wear new clothes and weapons;
frequent giving   makes friendships last
    if the purpose is pure.

A man should keep faith   with his friends always,
    returning gift for gift;
laughter should be   the reward of laughter,
    lying of lies.

A man should be faithful   to a friend
    and to the friends of a friend;
it is unwise   to offer friendship
    to a foe's friend.

If you have a friend   you feel you can trust
    and you want to win his heart,
open your mind to him,   give him gifts,
    and go to see him often.

If there's a man   that you mistrust
    and you want to win his heart,
let your words be fair   but false to your thought,
    pay back lying with lies.

Here's more advice   about the man
    whose intentions you don't trust:
laugh when he does,   let your words dissemble,
    give back gift for gift.

---

laughter should be. . . . This probably means mockery rather than good fellow-ship.

and you want to win his heart. Literally, "to receive good from him."

Always as a young man   I traveled alone,
　　and I would lose my way;
I felt I was rich   if I made a friend—
　　no man by himself is happy.

Men brave and generous   live the best lives,
　　seldom will they sorrow;
then there are fools,   afraid of everything,
　　who grumble instead of giving.

When I saw   two scarecrows in a field
　　I covered them with my clothes;
they looked like warriors   when they were dressed—
　　who hails a naked hero?

The pine tree withers   in an open place,
　　neither bark nor needles save it.
How shall a man   hated by everyone
　　live for very long?

Hotter than fire   friendship flames
　　five days among false friends;
then it dies down   when the sixth day comes,
　　and all love is lost.

You don't have to give   large gifts always,
　　small things often suffice;
half a loaf   and a lifted goblet
　　have found me friends.

On little shores   and little seas
　　live people of little sense;
everyone   has equal wisdom
　　where the world is half as wide.

Moderately wise   a man should be—
　　don't wish for too much wisdom;

the men who live   the fairest lives
  know just a number of things.

Moderately wise   a man should be—
  don't wish for too much wisdom;
a man's heart   is seldom happy
  if he is truly wise.

Moderately wise   a man should be—
  don't wish for too much wisdom;
if you can't see far   into the future,
  you can live free from care.

Flames from one log   leap to another,
  fire kindles fire;
a man learns   from the minds of others,
  a fool prefers his own.

Get up early   if you are after
  another man's life or money;
a sleeping wolf   will seldom make a kill
  nor a warrior win lying down.

Get up early   if you have few men,
  and attend to your tasks yourself;
much slips by   while you lie in bed—
  work is half of wealth.

How many roof-beams   and how much bark—
  a man can measure these;
and how much wood   will be enough
  to keep him warm all winter.

---

just a number of things. That is, not too many.
and how much bark. The bark is for the thatch. A lost stanza is conjectured
which would give examples of things that cannot be measured.

Don't be hungry   when you ride to the Thing,
  be clean though your clothes be poor;
you will not be shamed   by shoes and breeches,
  nor by your horse, though he be no prize.

Sniffing and searching   over the sea,
  the eagle watches the waves;
he's like the man   who comes among many
  but has few friends.

A man will ask   and answer questions
  if he wants to be called wise;
one man can know something   but two should not,
  the whole world knows if three do.

A clever man   will take good care
  how he shows his strength,
for he discovers   among the daring
  no man claims all the courage.

Often for the words   he says to others
  a man receives his reward.

To many houses   I came too early,
  to others much too late:
the beer was all gone   or they hadn't brewed it—
  unwelcome guests find no feasts.

At some tables   I was treated well—
  when I had meat of my own;
or when two hams hung   in a friend's house
  where I had eaten one.

There is nothing men find   better than fire
  or the sight of the sun,

where I had eaten one. The meaning here is "when I had paid back more than my share."

and to be allowed   good health
  and live a blameless life.

If a man's health fails   he may still be happy:
  some can rejoice in their sons,
some in their friends   or sufficient money,
  some in work well done.

Better to live   than to be lifeless:
  the living can hope for a cow.
While the wealthy man   sat warm by his fire,
  a dead man lay outside the door.

The lame ride horseback,   the handless drive herds,
  the deaf may be dauntless in battle;
better to be blind   than burned on a pyre,
  dead men do no deeds.

Though he be born   when you are buried,
  it's better to have a son;
you don't see many   memorial stones
  except those set by kinsmen.

Two things harry one;   the tongue is the head's bane,
  a man's fur coat   hides his hands.

Night is friendly   if you have enough food.

  A ship has small cabins.

  Don't trust the autumn night.

The weather seldom stays   five days the same,
  but it changes more in a month.

Two things harry one. The series of proverbs beginning here is an obvious interpolation, and occasionally enigmatic.

He who knows nothing   doesn't know this:
   money makes monkeys of men;
one man is wealthy,   another is in want—
   has that one no cause for complaint?

Cattle die,   kinsmen die,
   one day you die yourself;
but the words of praise   will not perish
   when a man wins fair fame.

Cattle die,   kinsmen die,
   one day you die yourself;
I know one thing   that never dies—
   the dead man's reputation.

I saw the full-stocked fields   of Fitjung's sons
   who now bear beggar's staves.
Don't trust wealth—   in the twinkling of an eye
   it can prove a fickle friend.

When a man is not wise,   he has only to win
   cattle or a woman's caress,
and his self-esteem waxes,   unlike his wits,
   he's all puffed up with pride.

He who would read   the sacred runes
   given by the gods,
     that Odin set down
     and the sage stained with color,
is well advised   to waste no words.

Praise the day at nightfall,   a woman when she's dead,
a sword proven,   a maiden married,
ice you've crossed,   ale you've drunk.

Cut trees when the wind blows,   sail in fair weather;
talk with maidens in the dark—   the day has many eyes.

Ask speed of a ship,   protection from a shield,
keenness from a sword,   from a maiden kisses.

Drink ale by the fireside,   skate on the ice,
buy lean steeds   and bloodstained swords,
fatten horses in the stable,   a dog in your home.

Never trust   what a maiden tells you
   nor count any woman constant;
their hearts are turned   on a potter's wheel,
   their minds are made to change.

A creaking bow,   a burning flame,
a yawning wolf,   a crow crying,
squealing swine,   a rootless tree,
billows rising,   a kettle boiling,
a dart flying,   falling seas,
new ice,   a serpent coiled,
a bride's bed-talk,   a broken sword,
a bear at play   or a king's boy,
a sick calf,   a willful slave,
sweet words from witches,   the newly slain,
your brother's murderer,   though met on the road,
a half-burned house   or a horse too swift
(if he breaks his leg   you've lost your mount)—
a man's too trusting   who takes a chance on these.

Never trust   a field sown early
   or a son too soon;
weather rules crops,   sons need wisdom,
   you run a risk both ways.

Thus you'll find the love   of a faithless woman:

buy lean steeds. Professor Dunn is no doubt correct in suggesting that the
horses should be thin because well-used, not underfed.

A creaking bow. . . . Stanzas 85–88, here printed as one stanza, are arranged
according to Vigfusson and Powell.

like a smooth-shod horse   on slippery ice—
a sprightly two-year-old   not yet trained,
or sailing with no rudder   in a frantic storm
or a lame man on an icy hill   running after reindeer.

Believe what I say—   I know them both—
    men don't keep faith with women;
we speak fair words   when we think most falsely
    to bewilder the wits of the wise.

Speak pleasing words   and offer presents
    to win a woman's love,
flatter a lady   about her looks:
    praise will have the prize.

Let no man ever   mock another,
    laughing at his love;
the stupid may be safe   where the wise give way
    to a fair folly.

Let no man ever   mock another
    for what so many suffer:
out of wise men   fools are made
    by the lures of love.

Only you can know   what lives near your heart,
    see clearly into yourself;
for the wise man,   no sickness is worse
    than nothing left to love.

I realized   as I sat among the reeds
    waiting for one I loved,
that she was both   body and soul to me,
    but no more mine for that.

I realized. Here through stanza 102 is told the sad story of Odin's love for
Billing's daughter.

I saw Billing's daughter   in her bed,
  a sun-bright maiden sleeping;
then all the earth   seemed empty of delight
  unless I could lie beside her.

"You must wait, Odin;   when it grows dark,
  come back if you want to woo me.
It would be unlucky   if other eyes
  witnessed my weakness."

So I returned,   thinking to receive
  delight for my desire,
persuaded that soon   I would possess
  her favor freely.

All for nothing: that night she had
  warriors barring the way;
they held burning torches   and brandished stakes—
  she had led me a merry chase.

When the sun rose   and I returned,
  not a soul was stirring;
I saw only the bitch   that sweet woman
  had bound to the bed.

Make no mistake—   there are many maidens
  fickle and false;
I learned this truth   that time I tried
  to lure one to love—
she made me suffer   every shame
  and denied me all delight.

Be happy at home   and gay with guests,
  but a man must have a mind.
Remembering much   and talking readily,
  he will be known as wise;

a nincompoop   never says anything
   because he's not very bright.

I sought the old giant,   and when I saw him,
   little I learned keeping still:
much I received   for the many words
   I spoke in Suttung's hall.

From her gilded chair   Gunnlod gave me
   a cup of costly mead;
an ill reward   she had in return
   for her quick kindness,
   for her heavy heart.

With a drill's teeth   I cut my trail,
   I gnawed right through the rock;
over and under me   wound the giants' ways—
   a perilous path I traveled.

From a good-looking bargain   I gained a lot,
   and so the wise lack little:
now the mead   that's the poet's muse
   can be drunk in human dwellings.

I don't believe   I could have come back
   from the giant's court
were it not for Gunnlod,   that good woman
   who lay in my arms for love.

The next day   the frost-giants found
   the High One in his hall;
they asked if Odin   were with the Aesir
   or if Suttung had slain him.

nincompoop. Translates *fimbulfambi.* Stanza 104 introduces a new adventure,
in which Odin obtains the mead of inspiration and makes it available to true
poets. The giantess Gunnlod gave him the mead at the expense of her father,
Suttung.

Odin didn't honor   his oath on the ring—
   what good is any pledge he gives?
Suttung died   of a poisoned drink,
   and Gunnlod grieves.

The Lay of Loddfafnir

I will sing   from the sage's chair
   by the Norns' sacred spring;
I watched and listened,   I looked and thought
   about the words of the wise
when they talked of runes   and what they reveal
at the High One's hall,   in the High One's hall—
   here is what I heard:

Heed my words, Loddfafnir,   listen to my counsel;
   you'll be better off if you believe me,
   follow my advice, and you'll fare well:
don't get up at night   except to guard the house
   or to rise and relieve yourself.

Heed my words, Loddfafnir,   listen to my counsel;
   you'll be better off if you believe me,
   follow my advice, and you'll fare well:
never lie   with a witch for love,
   or with locked joints you'll wake;

she'll cast a spell   so you won't care
   to be with men any more;
spurning meat   and every sport,
   you'll seek your bed in sorrow.

"*The Lay of Loddfafnir*." A separate collection of educational verses within the
Sayings of the High One. Loddfafnir is presumably a young man counseled by
a sage in the High One's hall, the advice being overheard by the poet—unless,
as Vigfusson suggests, this first stanza would introduce stanzas 138–155.

Heed my words, Loddfafnir,   listen to my counsel;
　you'll be better off if you believe me,
　follow my advice, and you'll fare well:
never lure   another man's wife
　to lie with you for love.

Heed my words, Loddfafnir,   listen to my counsel;
　you'll be better off if you believe me,
　follow my advice, and you'll fare well:
if you want to travel   over fjord or mountain,
　don't forget food.

Heed my words, Loddfafnir,   listen to my counsel;
　you'll be better off if you believe me,
　follow my advice, and you'll fare well:
never tell   a man you can't trust
　that you've lost your luck;
you'll be ill rewarded   if you think well
　of a malicious man.

I saw a man   stabbed so deeply
　by a wicked woman's words
her deceitful tongue   was death to him,
　yet all she said was a lie.

Heed my words, Loddfafnir,   listen to my counsel;
　you'll be better off if you believe me,
　follow my advice, and you'll fare well:
if you have faith   in a friend of yours,
　go to find him often;
brushwood and grass   will soon grow high
　on a road no travelers take.

Heed my words, Loddfafnir,   listen to my counsel;
　you'll be better off if you believe me,
　follow my advice, and you'll fare well:

rejoice in talk   with a man you respect
   and learn healing spells all your life.

Heed my words, Loddfafnir,   listen to my counsel;
   you'll be better off if you believe me,
   follow my advice, and you'll fare well:
always be faithful,   never be the first
   to fail a friendship;
grief consumes the heart   that must take care
   to keep itself concealed.

Heed my words, Loddfafnir,   listen to my counsel;
   you'll be better off if you believe me,
   follow my advice, and you'll fare well:
if you are wise   you'll exchange no words
   with fools you find on your way.

If a man's no good   he will never give you
   your rightful reward;
a worthy man   will help you to win
   favor and fame.

True bonds are formed   where men keep faith
   and don't hide their hearts.
Anything is better   than a breach of friendship—
   a real friend will say   what you'd rather not hear.

Heed my words, Loddfafnir,   listen to my counsel;
   you'll be better off if you believe me,
   follow my advice, and you'll fare well:
don't offer three words   to a man unworthy;
   good men come to grief
   when the worse make war.

Heed my words, Loddfafnir,   listen to my counsel;
   you'll be better off if you believe me,
   follow my advice, and you'll fare well:

don't make shoes   and don't make spear-shafts
  except the ones you use yourself;
a badly-fitted shoe   or a crooked shaft
  leads to bad luck.

Heed my words, Loddfafnir,   listen to my counsel;
  you'll be better off if you believe me,
  follow my advice, and you'll fare well:
when evil strikes you,   don't keep silent
  or let your foes find peace.

Heed my words, Loddfafnir,   listen to my counsel;
  you'll be better off if you believe me,
  follow my advice, and you'll fare well:
don't rejoice   in evil deeds;
  be glad to do good.

Heed my words, Loddfafnir,   listen to my counsel;
  you'll be better off if you believe me,
  follow my advice, and you'll fare well:
never look up   when you're locked in battle—
where many men   go mad with fear—
  an evil spell may strike you.

Heed my words, Loddfafnir,   listen to my counsel;
  you'll be better off if you believe me,
  follow my advice, and you'll fare well:
if you want to win   a woman's friendship
  and be in her good graces,
make fair promises   and fulfill them—
  who tires of treasure if he gets it?

Heed my words, Loddfafnir,   listen to my counsel;
  you'll be better off if you believe me,
  follow my advice, and you'll fare well:
I bid you be careful,   but don't overdo it;

watch out for ale   or another man's wife,
and don't let thieves   play you tricks.

Heed my words, Loddfafnir,   listen to my counsel;
  you'll be better off if you believe me,
  follow my advice, and you'll fare well:
don't mock a guest,   and never make fun
  of a man you meet on the road!

Those already arrived   are often unable
  to tell a newcomer's kin;
you'll never find a man   without a fault
or one so evil   he's no use at all.

Heed my words, Loddfafnir,   listen to my counsel;
  you'll be better off if you believe me,
  follow my advice, and you'll fare well:
never laugh   at long-bearded sages!
You may learn a lot   listening to the old,
and find wise words   in shriveled skins:
  among the hides hanging,
  among the pelts dangling,
  with rennets swinging to and fro.

Heed my words, Loddfafnir,   listen to my counsel;
  you'll be better off if you believe me,
  follow my advice, and you'll fare well:
don't scoff at a guest   or urge him toward the gate;
  be good to beggars!

That door must close   with a mighty cross-beam
  which opens for all arrivals;
lock it with a ring   or you'll receive
  rage as your reward.

Lock it with a ring. But the Cleasby-Vigfusson dictionary interprets "give a ring"
as advice to put a ring in the door for protection against evil.

Heed my words, Loddfafnir,   listen to my counsel;
   you'll be better off if you believe me,
   follow my advice, and you'll fare well:
the Earth's might can help you   if you're drinking mead.
Earth fights ale,   fire fights sickness;
choose oak if you're constipated,   corn against witchcraft,
elder for household strife—   the moon soothes hatred—
alum for cattle-sickness,   runes for misfortune,
   Earth fights floods.

Odin said:
I know that I hung   on a high windy tree
   for nine long nights;
I had a spear wound—   that was Odin's work—
   I struck myself.
No one can tell   about that tree,
   from what deep roots it rises.

They brought me no bread,   no horn to drink from,
   I gazed toward the ground.
Crying aloud,   I caught up runes;
   finally I fell.

Nine mighty songs   I learned from the son
   of Bolthorn, Bestla's father,
and I came to drink   of that costly mead
   the holy vessel held.

Thus I learned   the secret lore,
   prospered and waxed in wisdom;

"I know that I hung. . . ." Another source of Odin's wisdom is the runes he acquired by hanging himself on the Ash Tree and wounding himself with a spear. The details of this sacrifice have been interpreted as dependent on the Bible. This episode has no connection with "The Lay of Loddfafnir," although it interrupts it.

I caught up runes. Boer interprets "caught up" as "invented," "thought out."

the son/of Bolthorn. Possibly Mimir. The last two lines of the stanza refer to the Suttung episode.

I won words   from the words I sought,
   verses multiplied   where I sought verse.

You will find runes   and read staves rightly,
   the strong magic,
   the mighty spells
   that the sage set down,
   that the great gods made,
   wisdom of Odin.

Odin for the Aesir,   Dain for the elves,
   Dvalin for the dwarfs,
   Asvid for the giants,
   I made some myself.

Do you know how to write?   Do you know how to read?
Do you know how to paint?   Do you know how to prove?
Do you know how to wish?   Do you know how to worship?
Do you know how to summon?   Do you know how to sacrifice?

Better no prayers   than too many presents,
   gift ever looks for gift;
rather be forgotten   than fed too much.
Thus wrote Thund   before there were men
where he rose up   when he returned.

I know spells   no king's wife can say
   and no man has mastered;
one is called "Help"   because it can comfort
the sick and careworn,   relieve all sorrows.

I know another   which all men need
   who hope to be healers.

Odin for the Aesir. This stanza is about the making of runes.

I know a third   if I should need
   to fetter any foe;
it blunts the edge   of my enemy's sword,
   neither wiles nor weapons work.

I know a fourth: if I should find myself
   fettered hand and foot,
I shout the spell   that sets me free,
   bonds break from my feet,
   nothing holds my hands.

I know a fifth: in battle's fury
   if someone flings a spear,
it speeds not so fast   but that I can stop it—
   I have only to see it.

I know a sixth: if someone would harm me
   by writing runes on a tree root,
the man who wished   I would come to woe
   will meet misfortune, not I.

I know a seventh: if I see flames
   high around a hall,
no matter how far   the fire has spread
   my spell can stop it.

I know an eighth   which no one on Earth
   could fail to find useful:
when hatred waxes   among warriors
   the spell will soothe them.

I know a ninth: if I ever need
   to save my ship in a storm,
it will quiet the wind   and calm the waves,
   soothing the sea.

I know a tenth: any time I see
   witches sailing the sky

the spell I sing   sends them off their course;
   when they lose their skins
   they fail to find their homes.

I know an eleventh: if I lead to war
   good and faithful friends,
under a shield I shout   the spell that speeds them—
   well they fare in the fight,
   well they fare from the fight,
   wherever they go they fare well.

I know a twelfth: if up in a tree
   I see a corpse hanging high,
the mighty runes   I write and color
   make the man come down
   to talk with me.

I know a thirteenth: if I pour water
   over a youth,
he will not fall   in any fight,
   swords will not slay him.

I know a fourteenth,   as men will find
   when I tell them tales of the gods:
I always know the Aesir   from the Elves—
   few fools can do so.

I know a fifteenth   that the dwarf Thjodrorir
   chanted at Delling's door:
power to the Aesir,   triumph to the Elves,
   enlightenment to Odin.

I know a sixteenth: if I say that spell
   any girl soon grants my desires;

---

when they lose their skins. When witches fly, they leave their skins on the ground.

I win the heart   of the white-armed maiden,
 turn her thoughts where I will.

I know a seventeenth,   and with that spell
 no maiden will forsake me.

But all this lore   you, Loddfafnir,
 will long be lacking—
 though it would help you to have it,
 do you good to get it,
 be needed if you knew it.

I know an eighteenth   which I never tell
 a maiden or any man's wife—
the best of charms   if you can chant it;
 this is the last of my lay—
unless to a lady   who lies in my arms,
 or I'll sing it to my sister.

The sayings of the High One   heard in his hall
 are helpful to sons of men,
 harmful to giants.
Hail to the speaker,   hail the one he taught!
 They're lucky who have the lore,
 happy if they heed it!

THE LAY OF VAFTHRUDNIR

*Odin has a contest with the giant Vafthrudnir and proves him-
self the master of mythological lore.*

Odin said:
"Would it be a good thing,   Frigg, were I to go
   and make a visit to Vafthrudnir?
I've been longing   to match my lore
   against that giant's wisdom."

Frigg said:
"I would rather   Odin remained
   here at home with the gods;
I believe Vafthrudnir   can boast of being
   quickest-witted of his kind."

Odin said:
"Far have I traveled,   I've tried many things,
   against the gods proved my powers;
now I must visit   Vafthrudnir's home
   and learn how the giant lives."

Frigg said: .
"Then go safely,   safely return,
   may you rejoice in your journey!
Father of men,   may you find your wisdom
   surpasses the giant's skill."

Then Odin left   to test his learning
   against Vafthrudnir's lore;
the fierce one found the hall   of Im's father,
   and walked in without delay.

Odin said:
"Hail, Vafthrudnir!   I'm here in your hall
   to see what you look like,

1–6

I've come to find out   if they call you wise
    rightly or wrongly, giant."

Vafthrudnir said:
"Who is such a hero   he comes to my hall
    and flings bold words at my face?
You'll never leave here   still alive
    unless you're wiser than I."

Odin said:
"I am called Gagnrad,   I've come to your hall
    thirsty from my travels;
a weary wanderer   asks for your welcome—
    will you not greet a guest?"

Vafthrudnir said:
"Tell me then, Gagnrad,   why you talk standing—
    have a seat in the hall!
Then I'll learn   who has the greater lore,
    the aged giant or his guest."

Odin said:
"When a poor man comes   to call on the rich,
    he does well to count his words;
self-praise   wins little profit
    in the hall of a cold-hearted host."

Vafthrudnir said:
"Gagnrad, tell me,   if you'd rather try your luck
    with both feet on the floor,
what is the horse called   who climbs the heavens,
    drawing behind him day?"

Odin said:
"That is the sun horse,   Shiny-Mane,
    who brings the brightness of day;

he is considered   the best of his kind—
   the light never leaves his mane."

Vafthrudnir said:
"Gagnrad, tell me,   if you'd rather try your luck
   with both feet on the floor,
what horse comes eastward   climbing the sky
   to give sweet night to the gods?"

Odin said:
"Hrimfaxi, Frost-Mane,   draws forth night,
   giving pleasure to the gods;
drops of foam   fall from his bridle—
   that is the dew of dawn."

Vafthrudnir said:
"Gagnrad, tell me,   if you'd rather try your luck
   with both feet on the floor,
what is the river   which runs between
   the giants' land and the gods'?"

Odin said:
"The river Ifing   runs between
   the giants' land and the gods',
freely its waters   always flow;
   no ice can ever form."

Vafthrudnir said:
"Gagnrad, tell me,   if you'd rather try your luck
   with both feet on the floor,
on what field   will they meet to fight,
   the giant Surt and the gods?"

Odin said:
"Vigrid is the field   where they'll meet to fight,
   the giant Surt and the gods,

to a hundred miles   measured on each side
  the battleground has been marked out."

Vafthrudnir said:
"Guest, you've proved your learning,   take your place;
  come talk to me on the bench!
Here in this hall   let the loser's head
  fall to the winner's wisdom."

Odin said:
"To my first question   can you reply,
  Vafthrudnir, learned in lore—
what was the source   of the earth and sky;
  wise giant, how were they first formed?"

Vafthrudnir said:
"The earth was formed   from Ymir's flesh,
  rocky cliffs from his bones,
the frost-giant's skull   became the sky,
  his salty blood the sea."

Odin said:
"To my second question   can you reply,
  Vafthrudnir, learned in lore—
what made the moon   which looks down on men;
  what is the source of the sun?"

Vafthrudnir said:
"Mundilfoeri   is the moon's father,
  he is the sun's sire too;
each day they circle   around the sky—
  that's how men measure time."

---

a hundred miles. Here and elsewhere in the text, the Old Norse *hundrad* has been treated as a symbolic quantity; the word literally means 120.

Odin said:

"Answer my third question—   all men call you wise,
   Vafthrudnir, learned in lore;
whence came day   which looks down on men,
   night and the waning moon?"

Vafthrudnir said:

"Delling is the name   of Day's father,
   Night was born to Norvi.
The new and waning moons   were made by the gods
   so that men could measure time."

Odin said:

"Answer my fourth question—   all men call you wise,
   Vafthrudnir, learned in lore:
how were winter   and the warmth of summer
   given to the gods?"

Vafthrudnir said:

"Winter's father   is called Cold Wind,
   Summer's sire is Delight."

Odin said:

"Answer my fifth question—   all men call you wise,
   Vafthrudnir, learned in lore:
who was the oldest   of Ymir's kin
   who lived in the days long past?"

Vafthrudnir said:

"Uncounted winters   before the world was formed—
   then was Bergelmir born;
Thrudgelmir   was the giant's father,
   his grandfather Aurgelmir."

Delight. A giant, father of the sun.

Odin said:

"Answer my sixth question—   all men call you wise,
   Vafthrudnir, learned in lore:
how did he come   among the giants' kin,
   the ancient Aurgelmir?"

Vafthrudnir said:

"From the Waves of Frost   fell drops of poison
   which grew and formed a giant.
All our kinsmen   were so created—
   that's why they're far too fierce."

Odin said:

"Answer my seventh question—   all men call you wise,
   Vafthrudnir, learned in lore:
how did that stormy giant   sire his children
   without the help of a wife?"

Vafthrudnir said:

"They say that under   Aurgelmir's arms
   grew a boy and a girl;
between his legs   the giant begot
   a six-headed son."

Odin said:

"Answer my eighth question—   all commend your wisdom,
   Vafthrudnir, learned in lore:
what is the oldest,   earliest thing
   the all-knowing giant remembers?"

Vafthrudnir said:

"Uncounted winters   before the Earth was formed
   Bergelmir was born;
the first of my memories   is that great giant
   found in the flour-bin."

found in the flour-bin. That is, in the sea.

Odin said:
"Answer my ninth question— all commend your wisdom,
    Vafthrudnir, learned in lore:
whence comes the wind that stirs up waves
    but is never seen itself?"

Vafthrudnir said:
"A giant sits at the end of the sky
    clad in an eagle's cloak;
his moving wings are what make the wind
    that men feel on their faces."

Odin said:
"I'll ask you tenth— for you know all
    Valhalla's lore, Vafthrudnir,
why is Njord like one of the Aesir,
worshipped by men at many altars,
    when he wasn't born among them?"

Vafthrudnir said:
"Born to the Vanir in Vanaheim,
    he was given to the gods as hostage;
at the world's end he'll go home once more,
    return to his real kinsmen."

Odin said:
"I'll ask you eleventh, where do men take arms
    and fight to the death each day?"

Vafthrudnir said:
"The valiant warriors who wait in Valhalla
    fight to the death each day;
they bring the slain back from the battle,
    then they all sit in peace again."

A giant sits. . . . His name is Hraesvelg, "corpse-eater."

Odin said:
"Tell me twelfth   how you know so much,
  Vafthrudnir, about Valhalla;
about the gods   and the lore of giants
  you make no mistakes
  with your wide wisdom."

Vafthrudnir said:
"About the gods   and the lore of giants
  I can tell the truth,
  having seen all I say;
nine worlds I know   under Niflhel
  where the dead are sent to dwell."

Odin said:
"Far have I traveled,   I've tried many things,
  against the gods proved my powers—
who will be left   of living men
  when three winters see no summer?"

Vafthrudnir said:
"Lif and Lifdrasir   will both be left—
  they'll hide in Hoddmimir's forest.
The morning dew   will be their meat;
  they will beget more men."

Odin said:
"Far have I traveled,   I've tried many things,
  against the gods proved my powers—
how will the sun   cross the smooth sky
  when Fenrir finds his prey?"

---

when three winters see no summer. That is, at the Fimbulvetr which precedes
the world's end. See *The Sibyl's Prophecy,* stanza 40.

Lif and Lifdrasir. "Life," and "He who Wishes Life." They are descended from
giants, but benevolent.

when Fenrir finds his prey. That prey is the sun.

Vafthrudnir said: .
"Alfrodull   will have borne a daughter
    before she meets Fenrir's fangs,
and that girl,   when the great gods die,
    will ride her mother's roads."

Odin said:
"Far have I traveled,   I've tried many things,
    against the gods proved my powers—
who are the wise-minded   maidens seen
    flying over the ocean?"

Vafthrudnir said:
"Three times   their flights will touch the earth—
    those maids are Mogthrasir's daughters.
Their presence means   help and protection
    though they come of giant kin."

Odin said:
"Far have I traveled,   I've tried many things,
    against the gods proved my powers—
to which of the gods   go the Aesir's possessions
    when Surt's fires are spent?"

Vafthrudnir said:
"Vidar and Vali   will live in Valhalla
    when Surt's fires are spent,
Modi and Magni   inherit Mjollnir
    when the war is over."

Odin said:
"Far have I traveled,   I've tried many things,
    against the gods proved my powers—

the wise-minded maidens. The Hamingjur, especially helpful to women in child-birth.

Mogthrasir's daughters. According to Boer, Mogthrasir is the Lifdrasir of stanza 45, and the benevolence of giants is also part of the new world.

what is destined   to be Odin's doom
   when the gods go down to death?''

Vafthrudnir said:
"All-Father will be   swallowed by Fenrir;
   Vidar is to avenge him.
When the god cleaves   those cruel jaws,
   the Wolf will find his fate.''

Odin said:
"Far have I traveled,   I've tried many things,
   against the gods proved my powers—
what words did Odin   whisper to his son
   when Balder was placed on the pyre?''

Vafthrudnir said:
"There is no one living   who knows what words
   were the last you spoke to your son;
death was my witness   when I told the doom
   that lies in wait for the world.
All my lore   is less than Odin's—
   your wisdom will always win.''

death was my witness. Vafthrudnir was doomed because he was speaking to Odin; but also, he was speaking the truth because he was "fey," soon to die.

THE LAY OF GRIMNIR

Odin, captured by King Geirrod, offers good fortune and information about Valhalla to his rescuer, Geirrod's son Agnar, before avenging himself.

About the Sons of King Hunding

King Hunding had two sons; one was called Agnar, the other Geirrod. Agnar was ten years old, Geirrod was eight. The two of them went out in a rowboat to troll for small fish. A wind drove them out of the harbor. In the dark of night their ship crashed against land; they went ashore and found a farmer. They stayed with him over the winter. His wife served as foster-mother to Agnar, and the man took care of Geirrod.

In the springtime, the farmer got them a boat. When he and his wife were leading them down to the beach, the farmer said something to Geirrod alone. They had a fair wind, and came into their father's harbor. Geirrod was forward in the boat; he leaped out on shore, thrust the ship back, and shouted "Get out, and may the trolls take you!" The boat sailed away, and Geirrod went up toward the houses and was warmly welcomed. His father had died in the meantime. Geirrod became king and won great fame.

One day Odin and Frigg were sitting in Hlidscialf looking out over all the worlds. Odin said, "Do you see your foster-son Agnar begetting children with a witch in a cave? But my Geirrod is a king and rules the land." Frigg said: "He is so stingy with food that he starves his guests if he thinks there are too many." Odin said that was a great lie and they made a bet about it.

Frigg sent Fulla, one of her maids, to Geirrod. She bade the king take care not to be bewitched by a wizard who had come

---

The Lay of Grimnir. Many additional stanzas containing information about mythology or nomenclature were added to this poem, most of them of no particular interest. This translation includes only those stanzas which Boer indicates as authentic. Their numbers in the original are 1, 2, 3, 9, 10, 21, 22, 23, 25, 26, 45, 46, 47 (lines 1–3), 48 (lines 5–7), 51 (lines 1–2), 52 (lines 3–6), 53.

into his land, and said he could be recognized by the fact that no dog, no matter how savage, would attack him. It was not at all true that Geirrod was stingy with food. But he had the man seized whom the dogs would not attack; he was wearing a blue cloak and said his name was Grimnir but would say nothing further about himself when he was asked. The king said he would be forced to speak and set him between two fires; and he sat there for eight nights. King Geirrod had a son ten years old and had named him Agnar after his own brother. Agnar went to see Grimnir and brought him a horn full of wine to drink and said that the king did wrong to torment him for no reason. Grimnir emptied the horn. The fire was by that time so close that it was burning Grimnir's cloak. He said:

"Fire, you're too hot,   and much too fierce,
  take your flames further away!
My cloak is singed   though I hold it high;
  sparks fly against the fur.

Eight nights I sat bound   between these fires,
  denied all food and drink,
till Agnar came—   and he alone,
  Geirrod's son, shall rule the Goths.

You'll live happy, Agnar;   Odin, lord of men,
  will grant you all good fortune.
You won't again   for just one drink
  receive so great a reward.

Odin's heroes   know his hall
  as soon as they see it;
spears are its rafters,   shields thatch the roof,
  byrnies cover the benches.

byrnies – armour
chain mail

---

shall rule the Goths. "Goths" here as often means simply warriors.

Odin's heroes   know his hall
  as soon as they see it;
a wolf hangs over   the western door,
  above it an eagle hovers.

A river roars;   the great wolf's fish
  swims in the stream.
Deeper seem   the depths of Valglaumnir
  to men who must ford it.

Guarding Valhalla   a holy gate
  defends the inner doors;
ancient it is,   and few men know
  what kind of lock will close it.

Five hundred   and forty doors
  you will find in Valhalla;
eight hundred warriers   will use just one
  when they go to fight Fenrir.

The goat, Heidrun, stands   on Warfather's hall
  and bites off Laerad's branches;
the cask she fills   with clearest mead
  can't be drunk dry.

Eikthrynir the stag   stands on Warfather's hall
  and bites off Laerad's branches;
drops fall from his horns   down to the well
  from which the world's rivers run.

I have raised my eyes   to the gods above,
  and I'll soon have help

the great wolf's fish. The great wolf is Fenrir; his fish is the Serpent who swims
in the river surrounding Midgard (Boer).

down to the well. Hvergelmir, the well at the foot of Yggdrasil.

I have raised my eyes. . . . The translation of the first two lines is uncertain.

from all the Aesir   who'll come in
   to Aegir's hall
   to hold a feast.

My name is Grim,   my name is Gangleri,
   Herjan and Hjalmberi,
Thekk and Thridi,   Thund and Ud,
   Helblindi and Har.

Sad and Svipal   and Sanngetal,
   Herteit and Hnikar—
I've never been known   by one name only
   since I have wandered the world.

Too much ale, Geirrod,   muddled your mind,
   trusted friends betrayed you;
I can see   my own friend's sword,
   its blade all wet with blood.

Ygg will soon   summon the slain;
   your life won't last much longer.
The Norns are hostile—   you know I am Odin—
   come close to me now, if you can!"

[handwritten: Ygg – Odin for Yggdrasil]

King Geirrod was sitting down with a half-sheathed sword on his lap. When he heard that his visitor was Odin, he stood up, intending to take Odin away from the fires. The sword slipped out of his hand and fell, hilt down. The king stumbled and fell forward against the point of the sword; and so he died. Odin vanished. Then Agnar was king in that land for a long time.

My name is. . . . "Grim": Grimnir; "Gangleri": The Wanderer; "Herjan": Lord of Hosts; "Hjalmberi": Helm Bearer; "Har": The High One; "Sad": Truth; "Svipal": Changeable; "Sanngetal": Guessing-True.
my own friend's sword. That of Geirrod himself.

Skirnir's threats persuade Gerd, the giant Gymir's daughter, to accept Frey as her lover.

Njord's son Frey was at Hlidskjalf looking out over all the worlds. In Jotunheim he saw a very beautiful maiden as she walked from her father's hall to her own. From that moment on he was heartsick.

Frey had a servant called Skirnir. Njord asked him to try to get Frey to talk. Then Skadi said:

"Get up, Skirnir,   go and try
   to speak to our son;
find out why   Frey who has wisdom
   is now so sad."

Skirnir said:
"I can expect   an angry answer
   if I speak to your son,
trying to find out   why Frey who has wisdom
   is now so sad.

"Will you tell me, Frey,   foremost of gods,
   what I want to know:
why do you sit here   alone in the hall
   all day long, my lord?"

Frey said:
"Young Skirnir,   no words can say
   how heavy my heart is;
all day long   the sun gives light,
   but dark is my desire."

Skirnir said:
"Whatever your grief is   why do you feel
   that you must keep it from me?

but dark is my desire. This probably means "but I can't see her."

Long years ago   when we were young
    we learned to trust each other."

Frey said:
"In Gymir's court   I saw going by
    the one I love;
so white   were her shining arms
    they lit the sky and sea.

"No one ever   in all the world
    has loved a maiden so much.
Among the Aesir,   among the Elves,
    no one wants me to win her."

Skirnir said:
"Give me your horse   which will go through the dark
    ring of fiery flame,
and the famous sword   that will fight by itself
    against any giant."

Frey said:
"I'll give you the horse   which will go through the dark
    ring of fiery flame,
and the famous sword   that will fight by itself
    if a wise man wields it."

Skirnir said to the horse:
"Night has fallen,   now is the time;
    we'll cross the wet mountains,
    journey into Jotunheim.
We'll both come back   or both be captured
    by that mighty monster."

---

the dark/ring of fiery flame. Another instance of a mysterious woman surrounded by magical fire.
journey into Jotunheim. As in Boer.

Skirnir rode into Jotunheim and found Gymir's court. Savage dogs were tied to a wooden fence surrounding Gerd's hall. He rode to where a herdsman sat on a grave-mound and said to him:

"Can you tell me, herdsman,   as you keep watch
   looking all around you,
how I can manage   to meet the maiden
   despite Gymir's dogs?"

The herdsman said:
"You are either doomed   or dead already!
No matter what you do   you'll never meet
   Gymir's fair girl."

Skirnir said:
"Better to try   than be called a coward
   if you want to do a deed;
one day   I'll meet my doom:
   life is laid down before."

Gerd said:
"Who is making   that monstrous noise
   outside our door?
The earth trembles   under my feet,
   and Gymir's high halls."

The handmaid said:
"A man has dismounted   outside the door,
   his horse grazes on the grass."

Gerd said:
"Invite the stranger   to come inside,
   bring him a glass of beer!

But I am afraid   our unknown guest
  will be my brother's bane.

"Are you an Elf   or of the Aesir,
  one of the wise Vanir?
Why did you ride   over raging flames
  to reach this hall?"

Skirnir said:
"I am not an Elf,   nor of the Aesir,
  nor one of the wise Vanir;
and yet I rode   over raging flames
  to reach this hall.

"Eleven apples   all of gold
  I'll give you, Gerd;
you, in return,   need only reward
  Frey with your favor."

Gerd said:
"Eleven apples   will never be enough
  to make me change my mind:
Frey will never   enjoy my favor
  as long as we're both alive."

Skirnir said:
"I will give you   a ring of gold
  that burned with Balder;
eight others   equally heavy
  drop from it each ninth night."

Gerd said:
"I refuse   the ring of gold

my brother's bane. Apparently a reference to Beli, who was killed by Frey.
Skirnir can be considered Frey's alter ego.

Eleven apples. "Eleven" is probably transcribed by mistake from a similar word
meaning "of life," "giving eternal youth."

though it burned with Balder;
I need no gold   in Gymir's court
   where I wield my father's wealth."

Skirnir said:
"Do you see the slender,   rune-carved sword
   I'm holding in my hand?
I will hew   your head from your neck
   if you don't say yes!"

Gerd said:
"No pain   would have the power
   to make me change my mind;
but it's my guess   that if Gymir comes,
it won't be long   before the battle."

Skirnir said:
"Do you see the slender,   rune-carved sword
   I'm holding in my hand?
When he comes against   its cutting edge
   your father meets his fate.

"One touch   of my magic wand
   will make you mind;
maiden, you shall go   where no man
   will ever see you again.

"Where eagles perch   you'll have your place,
high above the world   you'll long for Hel;
you will find   your food more loathsome
   than the Serpent seems to men.

"You'll be a wonder   when you come out
for monsters to marvel at,   men to mock!

you will find your food more loathsome. These lines are dubious.

You'll be far more   famous than Heimdal;
  you'll gape behind bars.

"You'll rage and weep,   wailing for mercy
  as your tears swell with your sorrow!
Sit down and listen   to what I have to say
  of awful anguish,
    twofold torment.

"All day long   demons will pinch
  the captive in the giants' court;
thus you shall fare   in the frost-giants' hall:
  faint for food,
    cheerless you'll creep along.
But you can weep   as much as you want to,
  give back tears for torment.

"You'll make your home   with three-headed giants
  or have no husband at all;
    devoured by desire,
    you'll pine away in pain!
A dried-up thistle   thrust into a roof
  is what you'll look like.

"In the forests,   in fresh green woods,
  I sought a wizard's wand,
    a wizard's wand I found.

"Odin is angry at you,   Thor is angry at you,
  Frey's in a fury;
wanton woman,   you have awakened
  the grim wrath of the gods.

"Hear me, giants,   frost-giants, hear me,
Suttung's monstrous sons   and mighty gods—
I hereby forbid,   I deny forever

men to this maiden,
men to make her merry.

"The giant Hrimgrimnir   shall have you for his own,
    your husband in Hel;
there among the tree roots   wretched slaves
    shall give you goatpiss!
Nothing else   shall you ever drink,
    maiden, by your own will,
    maiden, by my will.

"I cut a giant-rune,   and carved three others:
frenzy, lewdness,   and lust,
but I'll erase   each one I wrote
    if they're not needed."

Gerd said:
"To your health, fair youth!   Accept this foaming cup
    filled with fine mead!
I never believed   that I could be
    so fond of Frey."

Skirnir said:
"I must not fail   to find out one thing
    before riding home from here:
how soon   will you come to stay
    with Njord's strong son?"

Gerd said:
"Both of us know   a place called Barri,
    peaceful and private;
let Njord's son go there   nine nights from now,
    and Gerd will give him joy."

Then Skirnir rode home. Frey was standing outside; he welcomed Skirnir and asked for the news:

"Tell me, Skirnir—   before you unsaddle
    or go one step further—
what has your journey   to Jotunheim
    meant for you or for me?"

Skirnir said:
"Both of us know   a place called Barri,
    peaceful and private;
let Njord's son go there   nine nights from now
    and Gerd will give him joy."

Frey said:
"One night is long,   two are longer,
    how can I think of a third?
Many times   one month has seemed shorter
    than this weary waiting."

than this weary waiting. The meaning here is conjectural; the last line literally
reads "than such a half-night."

THE LAY OF HARBARD

An argument between Odin, disguised as Harbard the ferry-man, and Thor, whose simplicity is no match for Harbard's sharp-tongued gaiety. The translation follows the very free meters of the original.

Thor was on his way back from the land of giants when he came to a narrow body of water. On the other side was a ferryman with his boat. Thor called:

"Who's the big boy   over there with the boat?"

Harbard said:
"Who's the stout fellow   I see across the sound?"

Thor said:
"Ferry me across,   and you'll have a fine breakfast—
the basket on my back   holds the best of foods.
I took time to eat   before I traveled,
stuffed myself   with herring and oatmeal."

The ferryman said:
"You praise your breakfast—   that's in the past—
   but you can't see what's to come.
Your house is dismal: I think your mother's dead."

Thor said:
"What you just said   would seem to all men
dreadful news—   that my mother is dead."

The ferryman said:
"It can't be true   that you own three farms,
you stand there barefoot   looking like a beggar—
even your breeches aren't whole!"

I think your mother's dead. Thor's mother is the Earth.
It can't be true. . . . The stanza implies that no one could care about the mother of so insignificant a person.

Thor said:
"Steer over this way! I'll show you where to land.
Who owns the ship   you hold there on shore?"

The ferryman said:
"For a great warrior   I work this ferry;
Hildolf is his name,   he lives on Radsey Sound.
He told me not to haul   robbers or horse thieves,
but only good men   who are known to me.
Tell me what you're called   if you want to cross."

Thor said:
"Even if I were outlawed,   I wouldn't lie
about my name and family: Odin is my father,
I'm Meili's brother,   Magni is my son.
It's Thor who would cross here,   a king among gods!
Now it's your turn—   tell me your name."

The Ferryman said:
"My name is Harbard—   seldom do I hide it."

Thor said:
"Why would you conceal it   unless you had cause?"

Harbard said:
"Even if I did have   you couldn't hope
to make me die,   unless I'm doomed."

Thor said:
"I'll be furious   if I'm forced
to wade through the water   and get all wet.
Little boy,   I'd pay you back
for jeering words,   if I could just reach you."

Even if I were outlawed. "Outlawed," here, means subject to being killed if caught.

Harbard said:
"Here I'll stand   until you cross the sound;
you'll find no one hardier   since Hrungnir died."

Thor said:
"You haven't forgotten   how I fought with Hrungnir,
the stout-hearted giant   whose head was made of stone;
I destroyed him,   he fell down dead—
what were you doing then, Harbard?"

Harbard said:
"I was with Fjolvar   five full years;
All-Green is the name   given to the land
where we fought battles,   felling our foes,
did many brave deeds,   made love to maidens."

Thor said:
"How well did your women treat you?"

Harbard said:
"They would have been gay,   had they been good to us,
they would have been wise,   had they been faithful.
They made string   out of sand,
  and the deepest dales
  they dug deeper.
My sharp wits   won them all;
  I slept with the seven sisters,
  and they were glad to give me pleasure.
What deeds were you doing then, Thor?"

Thor said:
"I killed Thjazi,   the courageous giant,
and threw the eyes   of Allvaldi's son
  to the high heavens;
I left them there to mark   my mighty works,
  as signs men will see forever.
What deeds were you doing then, Harbard?"

Harbard said:
"With mighty love-runes   I mastered witches,
 had them despite their husbands;
Hlebard I thought   a hardy giant—
 the magic wand he gave me
 cost him his wits."

Thor said:
"Ill return he had for a good gift."

Harbard said:
"An oak will keep   what it captures from another;
 every man is out for himself.
What deeds were you doing then, Thor?"

Thor said:
"I was waging war   against the giants,
loathsome hags   high in the mountains.
Good luck for Jotunheim   if they all had lived;
there would be no men   in all of Midgard.
What deeds were you doing then, Harbard?"

Harbard said:
"I was in Valland,   waging war,
goading the princes   to grant no truce.
Odin claims the earls   who fall on the field,
 Thor only thralls."

Thor said:
"That's the fair way   we'd get our followers,
 if you had more might."

Harbard said:
"Thor is brawny   but not very brave:

fear made you cram yourself   into a glove's finger—
  none would have thought you Thor;
so great was your dread   you didn't dare
sneeze or fart   lest Fjalar hear you."

Thor said:
"Chickenhearted Harbard,   I'd strike you down to Hel,
  if my arms were a little longer."

Harbard said:
"Why would you hit me   when I've done you no harm?
What deeds were you doing then, Thor?"

Thor said:
"I was in giant-land   guarding the river,
when Svarang's sons   searched till they found me.
The stones they hurled   did me no harm,
pretty soon   they were wanting peace.
What were you doing then, Harbard?"

Harbard said:
"In giant-land I met   a white-armed maiden,
lured and persuaded her   to a private place,
glad was the gold-bright one   to give me pleasure."

Thor said:
"The girl was good to you."

Harbard said:
"That was a time   I needed you, Thor,
  to help me hold the maiden."

Thor said:
"I would have helped you,   had I been there, happily."

fear made you cram yourself. This incident is also related in *The Insolence of Loki*.

Harbard said:
"I would have trusted you,   unless you tricked me."

Thor said:
"I don't bite heels   like a rawhide shoe in springtime."

Harbard said:
"What deeds were you doing then, Thor?"

Thor said:
"Berserk giant-women   I battled on Hlesey;
they did their worst   to bewitch all men."

Harbard said:
"Brave are you, Thor,   to battle with women!"

Thor said:
"More like wolves   were they than women;
they shattered the ship   I'd propped up on shore,
threatened me with cudgels,   chased Thjalfi away—
what deeds were you doing then, Harbard?"

Harbard said:
"I was right here,   waging war,
raising battleflags,   reddening spears."

Thor said:
"You mean the time   you came here to attack us."

Harbard said:
"I will atone for that   with an arm-ring:
arbiters will figure   what is fair."

with an arm-ring. An arm-ring sounds simply insufficient; but it may have another significance which would explain why Thor feels so particularly insulted
in the stanza that follows.

Thor said:
"Where do you unearth   such insulting words,
the most insulting   I ever heard?"

Harbard said:
"I find them among the old men who live in the hollows of
home."

Thor said:
"You give a good name to graves when you call them the
hollows of home."

Harbard said:
"So name I such things."

Thor said:
"Your loose tongue   will cost you your life
   if I wade across the water;
louder than a wolf   I think you'll howl,
   if my hammer hits you."

Harbard said:
"Go and seek out   Sif's lover;
what strength you have   better save for him."

Thor said:
"You say the words   you think will most wound me,
faint-hearted fellow,   but I know they're false."

Harbard said:
"My words are true—   your trip took you too long—
now you've wasted more time   standing here talking."

I find them among the old men. This strange conversation refers to Odin's get-
ting wisdom from the dead (as in *Sayings of the High One,* stanza 157). "The
hollows of home" accepts Boer's *heimishaugum* for Neckel's *heimis skógum,*
"the woods of the world" or "of home."

Thor said:
"Craven Harbard,   it's you who kept me."

Harbard said:
"I never thought   great Thor would be outwitted
  by a shepherd of ships."

Thor said:
"You'd better do my bidding   and row your boat
with no more mocking—   ferry Magni's father!"

Harbard said:
"Why don't you go home?   I'll never give you passage."

Thor said:
"Tell me how to go,   if you won't take me."

Harbard said:
"It's easy to tell,   and long to travel,
some distance uphill   and then down dale,
then take the left road   all the way to Verland;
there you'll meet   your mother Fjorgyn
who'll tell you how to find   your father's land."

Thor said:
"Will I get there within the day?"

Harbard said:
"You'll find it difficult   to get there by dawn,
since I think it's going to thaw."

Thor said:
"Short will be our talk now,   since you will only scoff;
I'll pay back your meanness   when we meet again!"

Harbard said:
"Get out of here, and go to Hel!"

THE LAY OF HYMIR

Thor goes fishing with the giant Hymir and defeats him in this and other contests of strength, so as to win a cauldron in which Aegir would brew beer.

The gods were happy—   they'd had a good hunt
and felt like feasting;   they found out,
by shaking small branches   steeped in blood,
that Aegir had everything   for brewing ale.

Meek and gentle,   merry as a child,
sat the giant   when Odin's son
looked him in the eye   and loudly commanded,
"You shall brew ale   to please the Aesir!"

Thor's tone of voice   vexed the giant;
Aegir resolved   to take revenge.
He bade Sif's husband   bring his own cauldron;
"In it I'll brew   the Aesir's ale."

And the great,   all-mighty gods
had no idea   what they should do
until good-hearted Tyr   turned to Hlorridi
with these words   of wise advice:

"On the eastern side   of Elivaga,
where the sky ends,   is Hymir's hall;
my giant kinsman   has a kettle,
a mighty cauldron   five miles deep."

---

by shaking small branches. This method of acquiring information was apparently familiar until the Christian era.

Meek and gentle. Follows Boer; the meaning of the first two lines is debated.

good-hearted Tyr. Not the war-god of the same name; the present Tyr is related to giants.

Thor said:
"Do you believe   he'll give us his boiler?"

Tyr said:
"He'll give it to us   if we use guile."

So they set out,   and that same day
were far from Asgard;   the giant, Egil,
took care of Thor's goats   whose horns curved high,
while the gods went on foot   to Hymir's hall.

There Tyr found   his fearsome grandmother—
she had nine hundred   ugly heads.
But a white-browed damsel   dressed in gold
welcomed the Aesir   and brought them ale.

"Kinsman of giants,   I counsel you both—
courageous as you are—   to hide under cauldrons.
I wouldn't be surprised   to see my sweetheart,
stingy with guests,   greet you unkindly."

And their evil host,   late coming home,
hard-minded Hymir,   returned from hunting.
As he came inside,   icicles clattered,
falling off   his frozen beard.

His mistress said:
"Hail, good Hymir!   Welcome home!
You'll find your son   sitting in your hall,
returned at last   from his long journey.
A friend to men   and foe to giants
is Tyr's companion—   they call him Veor.

"Look where they hide   at the end of the hall,
hoping a pillar   will be protection."
In front of the Aesir   the pillar flew apart,
fell to the ground   at the giant's look,

while from a cross-beam   eight kettles
came crashing down—   and one didn't break.
Then the gods   approached the giant;
Hymir faced   his great foe.

Nor was he happy   to see in his hall
the one who often made   a giantess weep.
He had three bulls   brought in at once,
commanded that they all be   cooked for dinner.

In haste each one   was shortened by a head
and quickly carried   to the cooking fire.
Sif's husband,   before he went to sleep,
all by himself   ate two whole steers.

It seemed to Hrungnir's   hoary friend
that Hlorridi   was a bit too hungry:
"After dinner   we'll all go out
to find enough game   to feed us three."

Veor said   he would row out to sea
if the baleful giant   provided bait.

Hymir said:
"Go to the herd   and help yourself,
curse of giants,   if you think you can!
No doubt you won't   find it difficult
to bring back an ox   we can use as bait."

Thor went quickly   into the wood,
and soon a black ox   stood in his way;
the giant-killer   caught the horns,
broke the beast's head   right off his body.

often made a giantess weep. Thor spent most of his time killing giants.
three bulls. Thor's appetite is also used for comic effect in *The Lay of Thrym*.
It seemed. . . . The division of stanzas 17 through 20 follows Boer.

Hymir said:
"You're even worse   when you're at work,
lord of the sea,   than sitting still."

Thor commanded   the kinsman of apes
to row still further   out to sea,
but Hymir's comment   made it clear
nothing could tempt him   to travel on.

Hymir, fishing   in a giant fury,
pulled from the water   two whales at once.
Odin's son, Veor,   sat in the stern;
his skillful hands   prepared the hook.

The bane of monsters   used as bait
the head he took   from Hymir's ox.
One who hates the gods   gaped to take it,
the hidden Serpent   that surrounds the world.

With a mighty pull   the friend of men
hauled the vile Serpent   right into the skiff;
his hammer crushed   the high-arched crest,
the foul head   of Fenrir's brother.

The Wolf roared,   rocks crashed together,
the whole world   moved at once;
then the Serpent   sank back in the sea.

While they rowed home,   Hymir, not rejoicing,
had not a single   word to say;
then he tried   another tack:

"If you are willing,   we'll share the work,
one to haul   the whales to the house
while the other secures   the ship on shore."

The Wolf roared. "Wolf" is conjectural for *Hreingalen*.

Hlorridi stood up;   he seized the prow,
lifted the boat   with the bilge still in it:
with all it contained,   oars, scoop, and cargo
he hauled that surf-swine   to Hymir's hall,
through woods, over mountains,   making his way.

And yet the proud,   pig-headed giant
was not discouraged   by such display;
"A man may look strong   rowing in the sea,
and weak when he tries   to crack a cup."

When Hlorridi took   the goblet in his hand,
and flung it, columns   crashed to the floor;
from where he sat   he splintered stone,
yet back to Hymir   they brought the cup whole.

The giant's mistress   gave Thor advice,
and what she told him,   in friendship, was true;
"Aim at Hymir's head!   It must be harder—
with all he consumes—   than any cup."

Then the stern goat-master,   Thor, stood up
and threw the goblet   with godly power.
As for Hymir,   his head stayed whole;
the round wine-cup   cracked and fell apart.

"A great prize   that I possessed
has gone forever   with that goblet."
And Hymir added: "But I must hold
still to the bargain—   your ale is brewed.

"There's one more trial   before you triumph:
can you carry   the cauldron home?"

that surf-swine. The boat.
the round wine-cup. The last two lines follow Boer's interpretation.

Tyr tried   twice to move it;
the kettle remained   rooted to the spot.

But Sif's husband   seized it by the rim,
strode down the hall   and out the door;
he hoisted the cauldron   to his head
and at his heels   the handles clattered.

They weren't far away   when Odin's son
turned back, wanting   one last look:
Out of his lair   came Hymir, leading
a host of giants,   many-headed.

Setting the kettle   quickly on the ground,
Thor swung Mjollnir,   the murderous hammer:
not a single monster   survived the blow.

They hadn't gone far   before they found
Hlorridi's goat   half-dead in its harness;
the swift runner   was lying still,
lamed in the leg   by Loki's craft.

You know that story—   let someone skilled
in lore of the gods   tell it at length—
how Thor received   as recompense
the boy and girl   that giant had sired.

The assembled gods   saw Thor arrive
carrying Hymir's   mighty cauldron;
thanks to his deeds   they all would drink
beer brewed by Aegir's   blazing fire.

They hadn't gone far. These two stanzas refer to another story, which occurred
in Egil's house (stanza 7). Thor used his goats for dinner with the giants, but
one of the guests, at Loki's suggestion, cracked the leg-bone. Thus the goat,
which should have been reconstituted with no ill effects, was lamed.

how Thor received. The last two lines follow Boer's interpretation.

THE INSOLENCE OF LOKI

Loki, the evil and sometimes comic genius among the Aesir, infuriates the gods and goddesses by evoking past scandals until he is finally quelled by the threat of Thor's hammer.

About Aegir and the Gods

Aegir, who was also called Gymir, brewed ale for the Aesir when they brought him the cauldron, as has just been told. Odin and his wife Frigg came to the feast. Thor did not, because he was in the East, in Jotunheim. Thor's wife, Sif, was there, and Bragi and his wife Idun. Tyr was there too; Tyr had only one hand because the Wolf, Fenrir, had bitten the other off when he was being bound. Njord was there, his wife Skadi, Frey and Freyja, and Odin's son Vidar. Loki was there, and Frey's servants Byggvir and Beyla. There were great numbers of the other Aesir and Elves. Aegir had two servants, Fimafeng and Eldir. Bright gold lit the hall. Cups filled themselves with ale. The place was a peaceful sanctuary.

Many people praised Aegir's servants. Loki could not bear that, and he killed Fimafeng. The Aesir brandished their shields, shouting at Loki, and chased him into the forest. Then they went back to their drinking.

Loki returned later and found Eldir outside. Loki said to him:

"Stop, Eldir,   don't take another step
    before you tell me this:
what say the Aesir   over their ale,
    here in this hall?"

Eldir said:
"About their weapons   and skill in war
    the great gods speak;

The Insolence of Loki. This kind of vituperative dialogue is called a *flyting* in Old Norse.

among the Elves and Aesir   drinking ale
  not one wishes you well."

Loki said:
"I don't intend   to be left out
  of Aegir's feast;
I'll bring the Aesir   to bitter strife,
  mix bad luck with their mead."

Eldir said:
"If you intend   not to be left out
  of Aegir's feast,
and befoul that hall   with hate and slander,
  they'll wipe the walls with you!"

Loki said:
"I tell you, Eldir,   if we two
  make war with words,
every time   you open your mouth
  I'll have an answer.

With that Loki went into the hall. When those who were already there saw who had come in, they all fell silent.

Loki said:
"Hopeful I come   to Aegir's hall
  from far away:
here is Lopt,   dying for a drink—
  won't someone bring me mead?

"Why so silent,   you gloomy gods,
  why sit there speechless?
Either invite me   to join the feast
  or tell me to leave!"

Bragi said:
"The Aesir will refuse   to make you room
  on a bench at this banquet;

the gods know well   what guests they want
    when they feel like feasting.''

Loki said:
''Odin, you told me   long ago
    when we blended our blood together,
that never again   would you take a drink of ale
    unless it was brought to us both.''

Odin said:
''Vidar, stand up   and give your seat
    to Fenrir's father;
or else we'll listen   to Loki's foul words
    here in Aegir's hall.''

Then Vidar stood up and poured mead for Loki. But before Loki
drank he said to the Aesir:

''Hail to the gods!   Hail to the goddesses!
    I greet the holy gods—
except for Bragi   there on the bench
    at this fair feast.''

Bragi said:
''I'll give you a sword,   a swift horse too,
    rings of gold to repay you,
lest you in anger   provoke the Aesir
    and feel their fury!''

Loki said:
''Bragi, you have   no horse to boast of,
    or gold rings to give;
among the Elves   and Aesir here
    none likes war so little,
    or flees a fight so fast.''

when we blended our blood together. How and why Odin and Loki became
blood brothers is unknown.

Bragi said:
"I tell you, were I outside   instead of inside
    Aegir's high hall,
I'd soon be holding   your head in my hands,
    you'd lose it for your lies."

Loki said:
"Loud talk   but little meaning,
    Bragi, jewel of the benches!
Why don't you fight   if you're so furious?
    Heroes don't hold back."

Idun said:
"I beg you, Bragi,   for all the gods,
    and for their sons' sake too,
don't tempt Loki   with taunting words
    here in Aegir's hall."

Loki said:
"Be quiet, Idun!   You, of all women
    the one most mad for men:
you have locked   your arms in love
    around your brother's bane."

Idun said:
"You've heard from me   no hateful words
    here in Aesir's hall;
too much beer   made Bragi talk,
    and I told him to keep quiet."

Gefjon said:
"Why should any   of the Aesir here
    fight with furious words?

and for their sons' sake too. This line is conjectural.

We know that Loki   likes nothing so well
  as making merry."

Loki said:
"Be quiet, Gefjon!   I will give you
  reason to rage:
I know a youth   who gave you a necklace—
  you laid a leg over him!"

Odin said:
"Loki, you're insane,   you've lost your mind
  to anger Gefjon;
she can tell   of times to come
  as clearly as I can."

Loki said:
"Be quiet, Odin!   You never could
  decide a fight fairly.
I know how often   you have allowed
  the weaker man to win!"

Odin said:
"It may be true   that I have allowed
  the weaker man to win,
but you spent eight years   beneath the earth,
  a woman, milking cows,
  and you have borne babies!
  I call that craven."

Loki said:
"Who chanted charms   on the Isle of Sams,
  who murdered by magic?

We know that Loki. . . . The exact meaning of this statement is debatable, but Gefjon must be thinking of how dangerous it is to be provoked by Loki's taunts.
decide a fight fairly. Elsewhere Odin explains that if he gave victory to inferior warriors it was in order to obtain the best for Valhalla.

In a wizard's guise   you walked the earth—
  I call that craven."

Frigg said:
"I say the deeds   you both have done
  are best kept quiet.
How the Aesir   acted in the past,
  forgive and forget."

Loki said:
"Be quiet, Frigg,   Fjorgyn's daughter,
  you were born mad for men:
Vidrir's wife   has wound her arms
  around both Ve and Vili."

*Vidrir – Odin,
Ve & Vili – Odin's
brothers*

Frigg said:
"If only I could see   in Aegir's hall
  a boy like Balder,
you'd have no hope   of leaving here
  before you took a beating."

Loki said:
"Frigg, would you like   to find out more
  of the wonders I can work?
I can boast   that you won't see Balder
  henceforth in any hall."

Freyja said:
"Loki, you're mad,   when you make known
  the evil you intend!
Frigg can see   what the future holds,
  she just doesn't say so."

I can boast. . . . Loki was responsible for Balder's death.

Loki said:
"Be quiet, Freyja!   That you're not faultless
   I have plain proof:
all the Elves and Aesir   assembled here
   have had you for a whore."

Freyja said:
"Your lying tongue   will turn back on you
   the evil charms it chants:
the gods are angry,   the goddesses too—
   you'll go home gloomy."

Loki said:
"Be quiet, Freyja!   You're a foul witch
   and brew baleful poisons;
the gods found you in bed   with your own brother,
   Freyja, when you farted."

Njord said:
"Who cares   how a few husbands
   came to be cuckolds!
But I find it strange   to see among us
   a god who gave birth to babies."

Loki said:
"Be quiet, Njord!   Everyone knows
   that the giants held you hostage;
Hymir's serving-maids   squatted over you,
   made water into your mouth."

Njord said:
"I am glad   the gods sent me east
   to be held as hostage:
the son I got there   no one scorns,
   the Aesir look on him as lord."

the son I got there: Frey.

Loki said:
"Njord, that's enough!   You've gone too far!
  I won't keep quiet any longer.
Your own sister   bore you that son—
  a wonder he's no worse."

Tyr said:
"Frey is the bravest   and the best
  among the Aesir;
he grieves no maiden   and no man's wife;
  he frees those he finds in fetters."

Loki said:
"Be quiet, Tyr!   No one could call you
  the perfect peacemaker!
Remember how   you lost your right hand
  to Fenrir's fangs."

Tyr said:
"I lost a hand,   but you lost the Wolf—
  those are equal evils;
because of me   your brother, bound,
  waits for the world to end."

Loki said:
"Be quiet, Tyr!   Your trusty wife
  is the mother of my son;
not one ring   have you received
  to soothe your shame."

Frey said:
"Chained beside the Wolf   to wait by the river
  until the gods go down,
you'll find yourself,   you father of evils,
  if you don't keep quiet."

Remember how you lost your right hand. The Wolf could not have been bound
had not Tyr put his hand in Fenrir's mouth.

Loki said:
"With gold you bought   the daughter of Gymir,
   and sold him your sword;
when the sons of Muspell   ride through Mirkwood,
   what will you fight with, Frey?"

Byggvir said:
"Had I so fair   a name as Frey,
   and such a home in heaven,
that evil crow   I'd crush to marrow,
   break every one of his bones!"

Loki said:
"Who's the wee creature   crouching there,
   sniffing and snuffling?
You must be always   close to Frey's ear,
   or grubbing about near the grindstone."

Byggvir said:
"My name is Byggvir,   but I'm called Brash
   among the Aesir and men;
I'm proud and happy   to be where Hropt's sons
   all drink ale together."

Loki said:
"Be quiet, Byggvir!   No one ever called you
   an open-handed host!
They couldn't see you   in the straw on the floor
   when the brave went out to battle."

Heimdal said:
"Loki, you're drunk!   You've lost your wits!
   Why can't you control yourself?
Drinking too much   will make any man
   say stupid things."

The sons of Muspell. Fire-giants who will ride through the mysterious border
domain called Mirkwood when the doom of the gods is at hand.

Loki said:
"Be quiet, Heimdal!   Fate has handed you
  a loathsome life:
bolt upright   you must always be,
  awake to guard the gods."

Skadi said:
"Wanton Loki,   you won't much longer
  feel your tail free:
the gods will use   your cold son's guts
  to bind you to a boulder."

Loki said:
"Perhaps the gods   will take Nari's guts
  and bind me to a boulder,
but when it came   to killing Thjazi,
  I was first and foremost."

Skadi said:
"If, when it came   to killing Thjazi,
  you were first and foremost,
from my house   and holy temples
  you'll have cold counsel."

Loki said:
"You spoke more sweetly   to Laufey's son
  when you lay beside me in bed.
There's a tale   well worth the telling,
  if we're all to air our faults!"

Then Sif came forward and served Loki mead in a crystal goblet. She said:

"Hail to you, Loki!   Lift the goblet
  full of fine mead!

Then one alone   among the Aesir
  you can find faultless.''

He took the goblet and said:
"You would be my choice,   could we believe you
  a man-hating woman;
but one at least   know it's not a lie
  to call Hlorridi cuckold,
  and that is your crafty Loki!''

Hlorridi = Thor

Beyla said:
"The mountains tremble—that must mean
  Hlorridi is coming home;
he'll know how to silence   the one who slanders
  all the Aesir and men.''

Loki said:
"Be quiet, Beyla!   Byggvir's wife
  likes to brew baleful poisons;
no one ever saw   among the Aesir
  a servant so foul and filthy.''

Then Thor came in and said:
"Be quiet, vile creature!   Or you'll hear a curse
  backed by the might of Mjollnir:
I'll strike off your head   with my heavy hammer,
  and you'll have no life left!''

Loki said:
"Now we see   Jord's son before us,
  tough-talking Thor!
But you won't be brave enough   to battle the Wolf,
  and he'll eat Odin.''

Thor said:
"Be quiet, vile creature,   or you'll hear a curse
  backed by the might of Mjollnir!

I'll pick you up and throw you   east to the giants—
  rid us of Loki at last."

Loki said:
"You shouldn't talk   of your travels eastward
  to anyone alive!
When the great hero hid   in the thumb of a glove,
  who would have thought him Thor?"

Thor said:
"Be quiet, vile creature,   or you'll hear a curse
  backed by the might of Mjollnir!
When my right hand strikes you   with Hrungnir's bane,
  you won't have a bone unbroken."

Loki said:
"I think I'll live   a long while yet,
  though you hold your hammer above me;
Skrymir's straps   were strong enough
  to keep your knapsack closed,
  and in perfect health you were hungry."

Thor said:
"Be quiet, vile creature,   or you'll hear a curse
  backed by the might of Mjollnir!
With Hrungnir's bane   I'll send you to Hel,
  to the Door of Death down below."

Loki said:
"I said to the Aesir   and to their sons
  just what I wanted to;
but now, Thor,   I think I'll leave—
  I'm quite convinced you'd kill!"

When the great hero hid. This episode is also mentioned in *The Lay of Harbard.*

"You brewed the ale, Aegir—   never again
     will you hold a feast in your hall:
may all that is here,   everything you own,
     fall to the flames,
          and drag you down with it!"

"You brewed the ale. . . ." It is apparently to be understood that Loki's farewell
gesture immediately followed the end of the poem.

THE LAY OF THRYM

Thor, disguised as Freyja, visits the land of the giants and recovers his stolen hammer.

Thunder-wielding Thor   woke in a rage—
someone had made off   with his mighty hammer;
his hair stood upright,   his beard shook with wrath,
wild for his weapon   the god groped around.

And these were the first words   Thor found to say:
"Listen now, Loki,   to what I have to tell you—
no one else has heard it   on Earth or in Heaven:
the god's hammer,   Mjollnir, is gone!"

They went to find   the fair goddess Freyja,
and these were the first words   Thor found to say:
"Freyja, will you lend   your feather coat to Loki?
To find my hammer   he will have to fly."

Freyja said:
"I would give it gladly,   were it made of gold;
I would not refuse   were the bird-skin silver."

Then Loki flew,   his bird-feathers whirring,
until he had left   the land of the Aesir,
until he was inside   the giants' domain.

Thrym sat on a grave-mound,   the king of the giants,
twisting gold   for his dogs' new collars,
trimming the manes   of his sleek mares.

Thrym said:
"How fare the Aesir?   How do the Elves fare?
What brings a god   to the land of giants?"

Thrym sat on a grave-mound. A position of eminence; Thrym was engaged in typical lordly pursuits.

Loki said:
"Ill fare the Aesir,   ill do the Elves fare;
have you hidden   Hlorridi's hammer?"

Thrym said:
"Yes, I have hidden   Hlorridi's hammer
eight leagues down   deep in the Earth,
lost to the Aesir   now and forever
unless they give me Freyja   to be my wife."

Then Loki flew,   his bird-feathers whirring,
until he had left   the land of the giants,
until he was inside   the Aesir's domain.

When they met   in the center of Asgard,
these were the first words   Thor found to say:
"Have you news,   or did you work for nothing?
Speak your tidings   now from the sky.
A messenger's story   is lost if he sits;
if he lies down,   he's sure to lie."

Loki said:
"Not without tidings   am I for my toil.
The king of the giants,   Thrym, has your hammer,
lost to the Aesir   now and forever
unless we give him Freyja   to be his wife."

They went to find   the fair goddess Freyja,
and these were the first words   Thor found to say:
"Freyja, you must dress   in bridal linen!
Then we will drive   to the giants' domain."

Freyja snorted   in such a fury
she made the hall   of the Aesir shake—
the Brising necklace   leaped on her breast—

the Brising necklace, possibly the work of dwarfs, is mentioned in *Beowulf.*

"I'll have gone mad   with hunger for men
the day I drive   to the giants' domain!"

Then the Aesir   came into council,
all the goddesses   talked, and the gods
in their wisdom   looked for a way
to lay their hands   on Hlorridi's hammer.

Then said Heimdal,   the radiant god—
he, like the Vanir,   could see into time—
"Let's dress Thor   in bridal linen,
give him the great   Brising necklace!

"A bunch of keys   we'll hang from his belt,
wrap womanly skirts   around his knees;
we'll pin bright jewels   upon his breast,
the bridal headdress   neatly bind."

Then said Thor,   lord of the thunder,
"All the Aesir   would call me craven
if I went wrapped   in the robes of a bride."

Then said Loki,   Laufey's son,
"Thor, give heed   to Heimdal's counsel;
giants will be soon   at home in Asgarth
unless your hammer   is in your hands again!"

Thor was clad   in linen clothing,
they gave him the great   Brising necklace,
they hung at his belt   a bunch of keys,
wrapped womanly skirts   around his knees;
they pinned bright jewels   upon his breast,
the bridal headdress   neatly bound.

Then said Loki,   Laufey's son,
"I shall dress   to look like your handmaid,
and drive with you   to the giant's domain."

Thor's two goats   were brought from their grazing,
rushed to the traces;   well they would run.
Mountains cracked open,   the Earth was aflame,
as Odin's son   drove on his way.

Then King Thrym   commanded the giants:
"All of you, stand up!   Put straw on the benches!
The Aesir have sent me   Freyja for my wife,
Njord's daughter,   from Noatun!

"Gold-horned cattle   graze in my meadows,
pure black oxen   for a giant's pleasure;
many are my jewels   and much my treasure—
nothing does my life   lack but Freyja."

It was early evening   when they arrived;
the giants sat down   to drink their ale.
One whole ox,   eight of the salmon,
the dainty dishes   meant for the ladies,
Thor consumed,   with three casks of mead.

Then said Thrym,   king of the giants,
"I've never seen a bride   with such sharp teeth!
Never did a bride take   bigger bites,
nor any maiden   drink more mead."

But the prudent   handmaid provided
this wise answer   to the giant's words:
"For eight days Freyja   has been fasting,
wild with longing   to see the giants' land."

The king bent under   the bride's veil for a kiss,
but leaped back in horror   the length of the hall:
"Why do Freyja's eyes   look so fierce?
They seem to burn   with blazing fire."

But the prudent   handmaid provided
this wise answer   to the giant's words:

"For eight days Freyja   has stayed awake,
wild with longing   to see the giants' land."

Then the giant's   hateful sister
dared to demand   a gift from the bride:
"Take from your arms   those red-gold rings,
if you want   to win my friendship,
my true friendship   and my favor."

Then said Thrym,   ruler of giants,
"Bring the hammer   and we will bless the bride.
Let Mjollnir lie   on the lap of the maiden
while we make our vows   in the name of Var."

Hlorridi's heart   leaped with laughter
then grew hard   when he saw his hammer.
First he struck   the king of giants,
then all Thrym's followers   Thor laid low.

He struck the aged   sister of giants,
bestowed on her,   as a gift from the bride,
a mighty blow   instead of money,
Mjollnir's wrath   for red-gold rings.
That's how the hammer   came back to Thor's hands.

and we will bless the bride. There are other instances of hammers being used
for consecration, although not specifically for marriage.

Speculation.
has it that Snori
Sturluson may have written
this himself

THE LAY OF VOLUND

Volund the smith, captured by King Nidud, hamstrung and imprisoned on an island, takes a terrible vengeance and escapes in the manner of Daedalos. This poem is one of the oldest in the collection and would seem to be Norwegian in origin.

In Sweden there was a king called Nidud. He had two sons, and a daughter whose name was Bodvild. There were three brothers who were the sons of a Finnish king. One was called Slagfid, another Egil, the third Volund. They were out on snowshoes after game. They came to Wolfdales and built themselves a house there. Close by was a body of water which was called Wolf Lake. Early one morning they found on the shore three women who were spinning flax. Their swanskins were lying beside them. They were valkyries; two were the daughters of King Hlodver, Hladgud the Swan White and Hervor the Wise, and the third was Olrun, the daughter of Kjar from Valland. The brothers took them home. Egil married Olrun; Slagfid, Swan White; and Volund, Hervor. They lived together for seven years. Then the valkyries flew away to go to battles, and didn't come back. Egil went to search for Olrun, and Slagfid looked for Swan White. But Volund stayed on in Wolfdales. He was the most skillful of men, according to the old tales. King Nidud had him captured, as it is told here.

Maidens flew   from the south through Mirkwood,
young and wise,   on their way to wars;
beside a lake   the southern maidens
sat down to rest   and spin fine flax.

One of them   embraced Egil,
the fair maiden held him   in her white arms;
another was Swan White—   she wore swan feathers,

on their way to wars. The literal meaning of the expression is "to weave destinies." Either is a more suitable occupation for valkyries than weaving flax.

and the third,   who was their sister,
wound her white arms   around Volund's neck.

So they lived   for seven years,
but the eighth   they started yearning,
and the ninth   could remain no longer;
the maidens wanted   to go through Mirkwood,
young and wise,   on their way to wars.

Slagfid and Egil   found the house empty,
looked for them everywhere,   inside and out.
Egil traveled eastward   searching for Olrun,
Slagfid looked for Swan White   in the south.

But Volund stayed   alone in Wolfdales;
he set red gold   with sparkling gems,
and bound all his rings   with a rope of bast.
So he waited   for his fair wife,
should she ever   come back again.

The Njara king,   Nidud, learned
that Volund lived   alone in Wolfdales;
he sent his men at night,   in studded mail coats,
their shields shone white   in the waning moon.

They dismounted   at Volund's door,
and without waiting   walked into the hall.
Bound together   on a rope of bast
were seven hundred rings,   the smith's treasure.

They took them off,   they put them back again;
just one ring   they did not replace.

The weather-wise hunter   came back home;
Volund was tired,   he'd traveled far.

Slagfid and Egil. Neckel repeats here line 1 of stanza 9.

He set bear steaks   to roast on the fire—
high blazed the faggots   from seasoned fir trees,
wind-dried wood,   warming Volund.

The master of Elves   sat on a bearskin
to count his rings;   one could not be found.
Hlodver's daughter   had it, he thought;
the wise valkyrie   was home again.

He sat there so long   he fell asleep,
and he awoke   to utter woe:
on his hands   were heavy shackles,
fetters were fastened   to his feet.

Volund said:
"What mighty warriors   mastered me,
left me bound   with a rope of bast?"

The king of Njara,   Nidud, called out:
"Tell me, Elf King,   how did all this gold
come into your hands,   here in the Wolfdales?"

Volund said:
"The gold was not lying   on Grani's road,
nor is my country   close to the Rhine;
I had a greater store   of gold and treasure
when I was home   with all my household."

He sat there so long. As Boer points out, Volund's behavior is illogical; if the valkyrie had come back, he would certainly not just have sat still by the fire. The ring, of course, is what gave his enemies power over him. Otherwise they would have taken all the rings, or none.

On Grani's road. Boer interprets this as meaning simply "out in the open," but it seems rather to suggest that "Njara" is close to Sigurd's country, while Volund found the gold elsewhere.

with all my household. It is not clear to what household Volund refers. It could be his father's home or, as Boer suggests, the home he had with the wife, not Hervor, mentioned in stanza 17.

Nidud's wife   walked into the hall,
stood before him,   and calmly said:
"No friend of yours   came out of that forest."

King Nidud gave to his daughter Bodvild the gold ring which he had taken from the cord of bast in Volund's hall. He himself wore the sword which had been Volund's. The queen said:

"He shows his teeth   when he looks at the sword,
or watches Bodvild   wearing the ring;
venomous snakes   have eyes like Volund's.
Cut his hamstrings   so he can't escape;
set him on an island   in the sea!"

So it was done. They hamstrung Volund and set him on an island called Saeverstad, not far from the shore. There he wrought all kinds of treasures for Nidud. No one dared to visit him except the king alone.

Volund said:
"A sword shines   at Nidud's side,
the one I sharpened   when I had most skill,
the one I tempered   as my skill taught me.
Gone forever   is that flashing blade:
Volund's smithy   won't see it again.
And Bodvild wears   what belonged to my bride—
I cannot get it back—   her bright gold ring."

He sat, never sleeping,   and swung his hammer;
wiles he wrought   to have revenge.

Nidud's two sons,   lured by the treasure,
came to the island   in the sea.

out of that forest. Two lines follow here:
    Hlodgun and Hervor,   Hlodver's daughters;
    wise was Ollrun,   Kjar's daughter.
Then the scene shifts to Nidud's hall.

They found a closed chest   and demanded the keys;
Volund, evil-hearted,   let them look in—
to their peril   he showed the princes
a glittering hoard   of gold and jewels.

Volund said:
"Come alone, you two,   another day!
You'll have such gold   as I can give you.
Make sure, my young lords,   you keep it a secret
from all the household   that you were here."

It wasn't long   before the two brothers
said to each other: "Let's go see the rings!"
They found the closed chest   and demanded the keys;
Volund, evil-hearted,   let them look in.

He hacked off   the two boys' heads,
buried their bodies   beneath the forge;
and the skulls   under their scalps
he bound in silver   and sent to Nidud.

He set their eyes   as precious stones,
and sent them to Nidud's   clever queen;
from the teeth   of the two boys
he cut breast-brooches   and sent them to Bodvild.

Bodvild praised   the ring she had broken:
"I'd be afraid   to tell anyone but you."

Volund said:
"I'll repair   the golden ring
so that your father   will find it fairer,
your mother will think it   much better,
and you will find   it fits as before."

Volund, evil-hearted. Meina as in Boer, rather than Neckel's *menia.*

Wiser than Bodvild,   he brought her beer;
soon she was sleeping   where she sat.
"Those who harmed me   have felt my hate;
one evil only   is not avenged."

"How I wish," said Volund,   "I could walk on my feet—
that was the work   of Nidud's warriors!"
Laughing aloud,   he rose into the air.
Bodvild, in tears,   went back to her home;
she wept for Volund's flight   and her father's fury.

Outside was standing   the clever queen;
then Nidud's wife   walked into the hall—
Volund had alighted   on the wall above—
"Are you awake, Nidud,   Njara's king?"

Nidud said:
"I sleep no longer;   all joy left my life
the day my sons died;   always I'm awake.
My mind has gone numb,   so cold was your counsel.
I only wish   to see Volund once more.

"Tell me, Volund,   lord of Elves,
what was the fate   of my two sons?"

Volund said:
"First, you shall swear   solemn oaths:
by the sides of a ship   and a shield's rim,
a horse's shoulder   and a sword's sharp edge,
that your hand will never   harm my wife,
that you won't be the bane   of Volund's bride,

"How I wish. . . ." Volund speaks ironically, since he now has no need of his feet; it is the return of the ring which makes his flight possible.

"First, you shall swear. . . ." Volund's courtesy to Bodvild is remarkable; he hardly seemed to think of her as his "wife." One is also surprised to find, at the end of the poem, that Nidud apparently honors this oath.

though you know well   the one I wed,
and we will have a baby   born in your hall.

Inside your smithy   at Saeverstad,
you'll see the bellows   stained with blood;
I hacked off   your two sons' heads,
buried their bodies   beneath the forge.

I took the skulls   under their scalps
and, bound in silver,   sent them to Nidud;
I set their eyes   as precious stones
and sent them to Nidud's   clever queen.

From the teeth   of the two boys
I cut breast-brooches   and sent them to Bodvild.
The only daughter   born to you both,
Bodvild, now   carries a child."

Nidud said:
"You never said anything   that grieved me so much,
that I so deeply   wished to deny.
There is no rider   tall enough to reach you;
no man is strong enough   to shoot you down
while you stay up there   against the sky."

Laughing, Volund   lifted himself aloft;
the sorrowful Nidud   sat there alone.

Nidud said:
"Get up, Thakrad,   best of my thralls,
and tell Bodvild,   the fair-browed maiden,
to put on her finery   and come to her father."

Nidud said:
"Is it true, Bodvild,   as I was told,
that you were with Volund   alone on the island?"

Bodvild said:
"It is true, Nidud,   as you were told,
that I was with Volund   alone on the island—
would I never lived   that unlucky day!
Against his powers   I could do nothing;
against his powers   I had none."

that unlucky day. This phrase is conjectural.

THE LAY OF ALVIS

Alvis tries to steal Thor's daughter, but is trapped into such a lengthy display of his knowledge that he is exposed to the morning sunlight and so dies. The poem amounts to a catalogue of literary synonyms.

Alvis said:
"Now I'll take my bride   and travel home,
   to my own hall's broad benches;
some may say   it's a hasty marriage,
   but I won't linger here any longer."

Thor said:
"Who are you? What's your name?   With that pale nose
   you must spend your nights in grave-mounds.
A loathsome monster   you look to me—
   you weren't born for this bride."

Alvis said:
"My name is Alvis;   under a stone,
   deep in the earth I dwell.
I have come here   to claim what's due me,
   pledged as a hammer's price."

Thor said:
"No promise binds me   to give you this bride;
   a father's word is final.
I wasn't there   when they offered you
   what one god only can give."

Alvis said:
"Who are you? Tell me,   what gives you the right
   to refuse me this radiant woman?

"Now I'll take my bride." The first and last lines of this stanza follow Boer's interpretation.

a hammer's price. The hammer is Mjollnir, made by the dwarfs.

You wander in   from who knows where—
  how did you get gold rings?"

Thor said:
"I am called Ving-Thor—   I've come from far away—
  and Odin is my father;
never will I let you   leave my hall
  to marry that maiden."

Alvis said: ·
"No, you will quickly   give your consent
  and do as I desire;
I've made up my mind—   that snow-white maiden
  must be my bride."

Thor said:
"You'll never marry   the Aesir maiden,
  wise guest, whatever your wishes,
if you can't answer   all I will ask
  of every one of the worlds.

"Tell me, Alvis—   dwarf, I think you know
  all that has ever happened—
what are those lands called   that men's eyes look upon,
  in every one of the worlds?"

Alvis said:
"It's Earth to men,   Fertile Field to the Aesir,
  to the wise Vanir The Ways,
Evergreen to giants,   to Elves Ever-Growing,
  the mighty gods call it Clay."

---

you wander in. Thor must have come home just as Alvis was preparing to leave
with his bride; "how . . . rings" is conjectural.
Odin. Literally "Long-Beard" *(Sigrani).*

Thor said:
"Tell me, Alvis—   dwarf, I think you know
  all that has ever happened—
what is the sky called,   the child of the sea,
  in every one of the worlds?"

Alvis said:
"Men say the Heavens;   the gods, Warm Shelter;
  the Vanir call it Wind-Weaver;
for the giants, High Home,   for Elves Fair Roof,
  for dwarfs it's Leaky Hall."

Thor said:
"Tell me, Alvis—   dwarf, I think you know
  all that has ever happened—
what is the moon called   that men can see,
  in every one of the worlds?"

Alvis said:
"Men say the Moon,   but gods, False Sun,
  in Hel it's Whirling Wheel;
for giants Speeder,   for dwarfs it's Shining One,
  elves call it Counter of Years."

Thor said:
"Tell me, Alvis,—   dwarf, I think you know
  all that has ever happened—
what is the sun called   which men can see,
  in every one of the worlds?"

Alvis said:
"Men call it Sol,   and gods the Sun,
  the dwarfs say Dvalin's Delight;

the child of the sea. Translated according to Bugge's emendation and interpretation.
Warm Shelter. This translation is conjectural.
Dvalin's Delight, literally "Dvalin's Plaything," must be ironic: Dvalin, like Alvis himself, is killed by the sunlight.

the giants Ever-Glowing,   the elves Fair Wheel,
   the Aesir Shadowless Shining."

Thor said:
"Tell me, Alvis—   dwarf, I think you know
   all that has ever happened—
what are the clouds called   that carry rain,
   in every one of the worlds?"

Alvis said:
"For men they are Clouds,   for gods Chance of Showers,
   the Vanir call them Wind Kites,
the giants Hope of Rain,   the elves Weather Makers,
   in Hel they are Helms of Hiding."

Thor said:
"Tell me, Alvis—   dwarf, I think you know
   all that has ever happened—
what is the wind called   that wanders far and wide,
   in every one of the worlds?"

Alvis said:
"Men call it Wind,   gods The Waverer,
   Whinnier the high gods say,
for giants it's The Shouter,   for elves Din-Maker,
   in Hel they say The Stormer."

Thor said:
"Tell me, Alvis—   dwarf, I think you know
   all that has ever happened—
what do they call   the calm that falls,
   in every one of the worlds?"

Alvis said:
"Men call it Tranquil,   gods say Anchorage,
   for elves it's Soother of Day;

Wind Kites. Literally, "Wind-Floating."

the giants' word is Calm,   the Vanir say Wind Lull,
  dwarfs call it Day's Refuge."

Thor said:
"Tell me, Alvis—   dwarf, I think you know
  all that has ever happened—
what is the sea   on which men sail,
  in every one of the worlds?"

Alvis said:
"Men call it Sea,   the gods Serene,
  for the wise Vanir it's Waves,
Eel-Home for giants,   Wet Runes for elves,
  dwarfs have named it The Deep."

Thor said:
"Tell me, Alvis—   dwarf, I think you know
  all that has ever happened—
what is fire called   whose flames men see,
  in every one of the worlds?"

Alvis said:
"Men call it Fire,   the Aesir Flame,
  for the wise Vanir it's Wave
giants say The Ravenous,   dwarfs call it Ravager,
  Hasty it's called in Hel."

Thor said:
"Tell me, Alvis—   dwarf, I think you know
  all that has ever happened—
what are the forests   found among men,
  in every one of the worlds?"

Alvis said:
"Men say Forest,   but Field's Mane the gods,
  in Hel it's Seaweed of the Hills,

Waves. As in Boer *(vág).*

it's Fuel to giants,   for elves Fair Branches,
   the wise Vanir say Wands."

Thor said:
"Tell me, Alvis—   dwarf, I think you know
   all that has ever happened—
what is the night called,   Norvi's daughter,
   in every one of the worlds?"

Alvis said:
"What is Night for men   the gods name Darkness,
   the Vanir call it The Veil,
giants say The Shadowy,   elves Sleep's Pleasure,
   the dwarfs call it God of Dream."

Thor said:
"Tell me, Alvis—   dwarf, I think you know
   all that has ever happened—
what is the seed   which is sown by men,
   in every one of the worlds?"

Alvis said:
"Men call it Barley,   the gods say Bear Grain,
   the Vanir name it High Growing,
the giants Edible,   the elves Beer Maker,
   in Hel it's Hanging Head."

Thor said:
"Tell me, Alvis—   dwarf, I think you know
   all that has ever happened—
what is the ale called   that all men drink,
   in every one of the worlds?"

Alvis said:
"Men call it Ale,   the Aesir Beer,
   the Vanir say Strong Drink,

giants say Cloudless,   in Hel they call it Mead,
  for Suttung's sons it's Feast Maker."

Thor said:
"I never met   another man
  so learned in ancient lore;
but too much talk   has trapped you, dwarf,
  for you must die in daylight.
  The sun shines now into the hall."

The birth and early adventures of Helgi, Sigmund's son, his meeting with the valkyrie Sigrun, and his defeat of Hodbrodd. The battle is preceded by a vituperative dialogue between Sinfjotli, Helgi's half-brother, and Gudmund, one of Hodbrodd's brothers.

The Lay of the Volsungs

Long years ago   while eagles shrieked
and rain streamed down   from the Hills of Heaven,
Helgi the warrior,   the high-minded hero,
Borghild's son,   was born in Bralund.

The Norns came   to the house that night,
those who would fashion   the prince's fate;
great fame, they said,   would mark his future,
he would be called   the best of kings.

Then they wound   the threads of fate—
while Bralund fortresses   fell to the ground—
gathered up the strands   into a golden rope,
and made it fast   in the moon's high hall.

East and west   they hid the ends;
the prince's lands   lay in between.

The First Lay of Helgi Hunding's Bane. The Helgi lays, fragmentary and confused in places, relate the story of Helgi, Sigmund's son, who is loved and protected by a valkyrie and, when he dies, visited by her in his grave. Later they are both reborn. In *The First Lay of Helgi* and *The Second Lay of Helgi,* the valkyrie's name is Sigrun; in *The Lay of Helgi Hjorvard's Son* she is called Sigrlinn. The narrative is interrupted from time to time by exchanges of insults between minor characters.
while eagles shrieked. The hero's birth was marked by portents of violence.
while Bralund fortresses. Sigmund was fighting in Bralund at the time of Helgi's birth. This line is translated according to Boer's interpretation.
the moon's high hall. The sky.

Neri's sister   went to the north
and fastened one end   to hold forever.

The son of the Volsungs   knew no sorrow,
nor did Borghild,   who gave him birth;
a starving raven   sat in a tree
and said to another,   "Something I know.

"In chain-mail stands   Sigmund's son—
now that it's dawn   he's a half-day old—
his eyes are keen,   as a king's should be.
When the wolf wins,   we'll have cause for joy."

The king's warriors   acclaimed his son,
people had hopes   for a good harvest;
leaving behind him   the din of battle,
Sigmund presented   a leek to the prince.

He named him Helgi,   and gave him Hringstead,
Solfjall, Snaefjall,   Sigar's Field,
Hringstead, Hatun,   and Himinvanga;
on Sinfjotli's brother   he girded a sword.

Helgi grew fast   among his friends,
a high-born hero   bright with happiness—
freely he gave out   gold to the warriors,
nor was he sparing   of bloodstained treasure.

He would not wait,   but went to war
as soon as he reached   his fifteenth year;

Neri's sister. Apparently one of the Norns.
knew no sorrow. Translated according to Boer; Neckel has "only one thing grieved. . . ."
When the wolf wins. That is, "Where men are slain we have something to eat."
presented a leek. The leek was a symbol of royalty.
Sinfjotli's brother. Sigmund and his sister, Signy, were Sinfjotli's parents.

he struck down   the dauntless Hunding
who long had ruled   over lands and men.

Hunding's sons   came to Helgi;
they said he must give them   gold and rings,
or else, they promised,   they'd pay back the prince
for battle-damage   and their father's death.

But they received   no riches from Helgi,
no wergild   would he award them;
he said they'd meet again   in a mighty storm
with bright spears flying   in battle's fury.

The princes fought   on a dueling field
laid out on an island   at Logafells;
when the foes broke   the peace of Frodi,
the hounds of Odin   hastened to feed.

Helgi sat down   when he had slain
Alf and Eyjolf   at Eagle Rock,
Hjorvard and Havard,   the sons of Hunding—
all his descendants—   the prince had destroyed.

A great light shone   from Logafells
and in its brilliance   lightning flashed.
The warrior saw   women riding
tall under helmets   at Himinvanga;
their shining byrnies   were stained with blood,
and from their spears   shot gleaming flames.

As soon as he left   the lair of wolves
Helgi asked   the southern maidens

the peace of Frodi. Frodi's magic mill is referred to *(Mill Song)* as a mill of
peace, but the reference is not otherwise clarified.
the hounds of Odin: wolves.
As soon as he left. The translation is uncertain. The first part of the line may
mean "early in the morning"; "the lair of wolves" may be a battlefield.

if they would go home   with the warriors
that very night;   they heard the noise of battle.

Hogni's daughter   leaned down from her horse—
the crashing shields quieted—   and said to the king,
"We are bound   for other business
than drinking beer   with you ring-breakers.

"My father means   to make me marry
the grim warrior, Granmar's son;
but I, Helgi,   have said that Hodbrodd,
famed for his courage,   is a feeble kitten.

"Soon he will come here;   he'll be my husband—
unless you are willing   to wage war
or make the prince   give up his prize."

Helgi said:
"Don't be afraid   of Isung's bane!
Unless I die first,   he'll have to fight."

The king sent   messengers to speed
over land and sea,   summoning warriors;
all that was needed   of the Niflung hoard
was pledged to bring heroes   and their brave sons.

"Tell them for me   to man their ships,
speed to Brand Island   and set out!"
Then the king waited   until they came,
a host of heroes   from Hedin's Island.

---

ring-breakers. A familiar kenning for a ruler or hero, referring to the gesture of breaking off part of a gold arm-ring as a present.
give up his prize. That is, Sigrun.
Isung's bane. Hodbrodd. Isung is unknown elsewhere.
the Niflung hoard. Here, the meaning is simply gold.

From Stafn's Ness   his fleet started out,
the great ships   adorned with gold;
Helgi asked Hjorleif   this question:
"Have you assembled   the dauntless host?"

The young hero   answered Helgi:
"It would be no short task   to count the ships,
slender-beaked,   with many sailors,
that starting from Trono   sailed out through Orvasund.

"There were twelve hundred   trusty men,
and half again   as many in Hatun:
the king's warriors   keen for battle."

The captain ordered   the tents taken down
so that the warriors   would awaken;
the dauntless heroes   saw day's first light.
Then they were ready   to raise the sails;
the fleet set out   from the Firth of Varin.

Oars splashed,   iron grated,
shield rang on shield   as the Vikings rowed,
cutting through waves   at the king's command,
further and further   the fleet sped on.

The sound that came   from the long keels
crashing against   the crested waves
was the boom of surf   that breaks on rocks.

Helgi said to hoist   the tall sail higher;
they would come through   the crowding waves,
even when those dread   daughters of Aegir
reached up, trying   to wreck the ships.

---

the tents taken down. The "tents" are the awnings under which the warriors
slept on the ships. Line 2 is debatable.

Sigrun the valkyrie,   above them in the sky,
rescued the ships   and saved the warriors,
wrenched from Ran's hands   the horses of the deep,
and turned their prows   toward Gnipagrove.

When evening came   in Una Bay
the king's fair fleet   floated close to shore;
men stood   at Svarin's Cairn
with wrathful hearts,   and watched the host.

High-born Gudmund   gave them this greeting:
"What king   commands this fleet,
who leads these warriors   to our land?"

Sinfjotli answered,   raising to the sail-yard
the red war shield   whose rim was gold—
he was a lookout   well able to reply,
no lord would find him   at a loss for words:

"When you go home   to feed your hounds,
when you summon   the swine to the swill,
say that the Volsungs   have sailed from the east,
fearful of nothing   in Gnipagrove.

"Hodbrodd will find   Helgi here,
the flight-hating chieftain,   among his fleet;
where he fights,   eagles eat their fill
while you hide in corners   kissing slavegirls."

Gudmund said:
"Little you remember   the old lore,
prince; when you talk   you lie in your teeth!

"When you go home. . . ." The implication of the first two lines is uncertain;
Sinfjotli seems to be calling Gudmund menial.
the old lore. Gudmund refers to the stories of Sigmund and Sinfjotli when they
roamed the forests together. Sinfjotli killed his half-brothers to avenge his
mother.

What wolves delight in   you have devoured,
you have been   your brothers' bane,
your chill lips   love to suck wounds,
you have crawled home   to loathsome caves."

Sinfjotli said:
"You were a witch   of Varin's Isle,
a woman who lied   with every word.
No warrior   could win your love;
you would have no man   except myself.

"You were the vile hag,   the dread valkyrie,
hateful, loathsome,   in Odin's hall
where the dead warriors   would have waged war,
false woman,   to win your favor.

Nine wolves   you brought into the world
on Saga Ness—   and I sired them all."

Gudmund said:
"You never fathered   wolves like Fenrir,
oldest of all,   that I remember;
you were gelded   by giant maidens
on Thor's Ness   near Gnipagrove.

Siggeir's stepson,   you crawled into caves,
glad for the wolf songs   loud in the woods;
all kinds of horror   came from your hands—
you broke open   your brothers' breasts,
you won great fame   for fearful deeds."

Sinfjotli said:
"In Brafield you were   Grani's bride,
gold-bitted,   good at galloping;
I've made you speed, hag,   until you couldn't stand,
slender in girth,   and going downhill."

slender in girth. . . . The meaning of this line is uncertain.

"Once you looked like   a loutish boy,
when you were milking   Gullnir's goats;
but another day   you were Imd's daughter
in tattered rags—shall I tell you more?"

Gudmund said:
"Ravens will feed   at Freka Stone—
I'll delight them   with your dead body—
before I summon   swine to the swill
or your dogs either,   devils take you!"

Helgi said:
"Sinfjotli, it would be   much more fitting
to fight with men   and feed the eagles.
What's the use   of insulting words
even when ring-breakers   burn with rage!

"I expect no good   from Granmar's sons,
but worthy chieftains   won't twist the truth:
they made it clear   at Moinsheim
that they have the spirit   to use their swords."

In great haste   on their swift horses,
Svidpud and Sveggjud,   they went to Solheim
through dewy valleys,   over dark mountains;
the earth trembled   where the princes trod.

They met the king   at the courtyard gate,
told him that warriors   were on their way.
Hodbrodd stood outside   wearing a helmet,
he knew on sight   who the horsemen were:
"Why is there such fury   in your faces?"

---

the earth trembled. This line contains the untranslated words *mistar marr,*
which may mean "sea of clouds" or "sea of mist"; or else it may refer to a
valkyrie named Mist, or to her horse.

Orr said:
"Powerful ships   have come to our shores,
masted stags   with tall sails,
there are many shields   and oars scraped smooth,
a mighty crew   of cheerful Volsungs.

"Fifteen thousand   are on shore already,
seven thousand more   are out in the Sogn;
their boats are anchored   at Gnipagrove,
raven-black surf-beasts   blazoned with gold.
The larger part   of his host has landed:
Helgi won't wait   to start the war."

Hodbrodd said:
"To the great council!   Gallop all the way!
Sporvitnir   to Sparin's Heath,
Melnir, Mylnir,   go to Mirkwood!
Let no one stay   sitting at home
if he has the strength   to wield a sword.

"Summon Hogni,   the sons of Hring,
Atli and Yngvi,   Alf the Old;
with such brave men,   eager for battle,
we'll make little   of the Volsung might!"

With one sweeping turn   as spears clashed together
they met to fight   at Freka Stone;
ever was Helgi,   Hunding's bane,
in front of the host   where battle was hottest,
eager for the fray   and hating flight—
this was a man   with a mighty heart.

The warrior maidens   who watched over Helgi
swept down from the sky   as spears rang louder;

masted stags: ships.
with a mighty heart. The word translated by "heart" here means literally "mood-acorn."

these words spoke Sigrun,   the wound-wise Valkyrie,
while wolves were feasting   on ravens' food:

"Long life to the prince!   Be glad and prosper,
a rightful king   commanding hosts;
you have felled   the flight-hating lord,
Hodbrodd, the bane   of baleful foes.

"Prince, you shall have   a worthy prize:
red-gold rings   and a royal maiden.
In health and happiness   you shall have
Hogni's daughter   and Hringstead too,
triumph and lands;   the fight is finished."

the fight is finished. Boer does not include these words in Sigrun's speech.

THE LAY OF HELGI HJORVARD'S SON

A series of fragments from the Helgi story relating events preceding the hero's birth, his naming by the valkyrie Svava, the exchange of insults between Helgi's companion Atli and the giant Hati's daughter, the mortally wounded Helgi's last conversation with Svava in which he leaves her to his brother Hedin.

About Hjorvard and Sigrlinn

There was a king named Hjorvard. He had four wives. Alfhild was the mother of his son Hedin, Saereid was the mother of Humlung, Sinrjod was the mother of Hymling. King Hjorvard had sworn that he would marry the most beautiful woman he could find. He learned that King Svafnir's daughter was the fairest of women; her name was Sigrlinn.

Atli, the son of Hjorvard's earl Idmund, went to ask King Svafnir for Sigrlinn's hand. He spent the whole winter at Svafnir's court. There was an earl named Franmar who was Sigrlinn's foster-father; he had a daughter called Alof. The earl advised that the maiden not be given to Hjorvard, and Atli returned home.

One day Atli, the earl's son, was standing near a certain grove of trees. A bird in the branches above him had heard the king's men saying that Hjorvard's wives were the fairest of women. The bird twittered and Atli understood what he said:

"Have you seen Sigrlinn,   Svafnir's daughter,
the fairest maiden   in Munarheim?
—yet no one can find   a fault in the women
Hjorvard has   at home in Glasirgrove."

Atli said:
"I am Atli,   Idmund's son;
wise bird,   will you tell me more?"

The bird said:
"I'll speak if the warrior   will sacrifice to me,
and let me have   what my heart desires."

Atli said:
"Don't ask for Hjorvard   or any of his sons,
or for his brides,   the beautiful women
the king married,   who live at his court.
Let's bargain fairly,   as befits friends!"

The bird said:
"My price will be temples   and holy places,
gold-horned cattle   from Hjorvard's pastures,
once he has Sigrlinn   safe in his arms
and she consents   to follow the king."

This happened before Atli went on his journey. When he returned home and the king asked him the news he said:

"We've had no triumph   for all our toil;
our horses struggled   over stony mountains,
waded through   the Saemon's waters;
then we were denied   Svafnir's daughter,
rich in rings.   She will not be your wife."

The king said that they should try again. He went himself. When they reached the top of the mountains they saw great fires raging in Svavaland and clouds of dust coming from horses' hoofs. The king rode down into the valley and set up camp for the night near a river. Atli kept watch and crossed the river. He found a house. A large bird sat guarding it, fast asleep. Atli killed the bird with his spear. Inside the house he found Sigrlinn the king's daughter and Alof the earl's daughter, and took them away with him. Earl Franmar had changed himself into an eagle, and they had been kept out of the way of the battle by sorcery.

A king named Hrodmar, Sigrlinn's suitor, had killed King Svafnir and plundered and burned the land.

King Hjorvard married Sigrlinn and Atli married Alof.

Hjorvard and Sigrlinn had a strong and handsome son. He never spoke much, and no name would stick to him. He was

sitting on a grave-mound when he saw nine valkyries riding.
The noblest-looking of them said:

"Helgi the warrior,   you'll wait a long time
to own gold rings   or Rodulsfells
if you keep silence,   though eagles shrieked early,
prince, and of courage   you give proof."

Helgi said:
"What gift shall I have   with the name of Helgi
which you, fair woman,   have found for me?
Take your time   before you tell me!
That name won't be mine   unless you are too."

The valkyrie said:
"There are swords hidden   in Sigarsholm,
four more   would make them fifty;
one of those blades   is the best of all,
the bane of armor,   bound with gold.

"On its hilt a peace ring,   heart in the steel,
its tip strikes terror—   who takes the sword wins these—
over the blade   winds a bloodstained serpent,
along it twists   a snake's long tail."

King Eylimi had a daughter called Svava. She was a valkyrie,
and rode through the air and over the sea. It was she who gave
Helgi his name, and afterwards she often helped him in battles.

Helgi said:
"Hjorvard, you will not be   known for your wisdom,
though the hosts follow you   and you have fame;

though eagles shrieked early. A reference to the portents attending Helgi's
birth.
on its hilt a peace ring. Through this ring ran straps which were wound around
the scabbard when the sword was not in use.
a snake's long tail. This design was on an unidentified part of the sword.

at your command fire   consumed that kingdom
where they had done   no damage to you.

"But King Hrodmar   holds the rings,
those which our kinsmen   used to claim;
without a foe   left for him to fear,
he thinks he's the master   of dead men's gold."

Hjorvard answered that he would give Helgi men to help him
avenge his mother's father. Then Helgi went to find the sword
Svava had told him about. After that he and Atli set out together
and killed Hrodmar and did many daring deeds.

He killed the giant Hati, who was sitting on a cliff. Helgi and
Atli anchored in Hatafjord. Atli kept watch during the first part
of the night.

Hrimgerd, Hati's daughter, said:
"What heroes have come   to Hatafjord?
Shields are hung   for tents on your ships;
few things on Earth   I think you'd fear—
    what do you call your king?"

Atli said:
"His name is Helgi,   and there's no harm
    a witch can do that warrior;
the king's fleet   is an iron fortress
    no hag can harry."

Hrimgerd said:
"What do they call you,   mighty man,
    by what name are you known?
The prince must trust you   if your place
    is the forecastle of his fair ship."

Shields are hung. Shields used instead of tents showed the warlike intention of
Helgi's men, who would thus be instantly ready for battle.
the forecastle of his fair ship. The place of greatest responsibility.

Atli said:
"You'll find Atli   no friend at all—
    I've little love for witches;
from a ship's wet prow   I've watched them on their wolves,
    and many times made them suffer.

What do they call you,   corpse-hungry hag?
    Witch, who was your father?
You should be buried   nine leagues below the earth,
    growing barley on your breast."

Hrimgerd said:
"My name is Hrimgerd,   Hati was my father—
    the greatest of all the giants;
he had captured   countless women
    when Helgi killed him."

Atli said:
"Witch, you stood   in front of Helgi's ship,
    and blocked the bay against him;
the prince's warriors   would all have been Ran's prey,
    if a spear hadn't stopped you."

Hrimgerd said:
"Atli, you are blind!   What you believe
    you must have dreamed in the dark.
It was my mother   who held the hero's ships,
    I drowned Hlodvard's sons in the sea.

"Well might you neigh   if you weren't gelded—
    Hrimgerd tosses her tail;
I think the hero's backside   bears his heart,
    though he makes sounds like a stallion."

You'll find Atli. . . . The original here contains a pun on "Atli" and *atall*, "fierce."
Hlodvard's sons. Nothing further is known of these.

Atli said:

"I'd be stallion enough   if I stepped on shore
   and made you feel my strength;
were I to bother,   you'd be beaten—
   how high your tail then, Hrimgerd?"

Hrimgerd said:

"Come ashore, Atli,   if you're strong enough,
   I'll be in Varin's Bay.
Warrior, you'll see   your ribs pulled straight,
   if I get you in my grip!"

Atli said:

"I'll stand my watch   till the men awake
   and they can protect the prince;
I wouldn't be surprised   to see a witch
   rise up beneath our bottom."

Hrimgerd said:

"Wake up, Helgi,   you're in Hrimgerd's debt—
   your hand struck down Hati;
one night in bed   as the prince's bride
   and I'll be quite content."

Helgi said:

"Lodin will lie with you,   loathsome as you are,
   Tholl is the hairy one's home;
he's very wise   and the worst of giants,
   a man fit for you to marry."

Hrimgerd said:

"Helgi would prefer the one   who watched the harbor
   all night among the men;
a shining maiden,   mightier than I,
   she stepped ashore from the sea—
   that's how your fleet was made fast.

It's her fault   that Hrimgerd failed
  to kill the king's men."

Helgi said:
"Hrimgerd, I'll give you   something for your grief,
  but you must tell me more:
did one valkyrie   visit my ship,
  or did many travel together?"

Hrimgerd said:
"Three times nine they came,   but one commanded,
  a white maid wearing a helmet;
from the horses' manes   as they tossed their heads,
  dew ran down to valleys,
  high forests had hail,
  fruitful were the fields below—
  all this I looked at and loathed."

Atli said:
"Turn your eyes east, Hrimgerd,   Helgi's runes
  have brought you down to death;
at sea or in harbor   the fleet is safe,
  and the warriors with it too.

"It's day now, Hrimgerd,   Atli delayed you—
  now you must face your fate:
you'll mark the harbor   and make men laugh
  when they see you turned to stone."

King Helgi was a great warrior. He visited King Eylimi and
asked for the hand of his daughter Svava.   Helgi and Svava
exchanged vows, and the love between them was very great.
Svava stayed at home with her father while Helgi waged war.
Svava was still a valkyrie as before.

"It's day now, Hrimgerd." Another instance of the malevolence of daylight for
monsters of various kinds. This speech may belong to Helgi.

Hedin was at home with his father King Hjorvard in Norway. He was returning alone from the woods on Yule Eve when he met a troll-woman. She was riding a wolf and had snakes for reins. She offered to stay with Hedin.

"No," he said. She said, "You'll pay for this when you drink from the toasting-cup."

That evening the men were making vows. A sacrificial boar was led forward; they laid their hands on it and made vows as they drank from the toasting-cup. Hedin swore that he would have Svava, Eylimi's daughter, the beloved of Helgi, his brother. Then he regretted his vow so much that he went away, following the wild paths southward over the countryside until he found Helgi.

Helgi said:
"Hail to you, Hedin! What brings you here?
What news do you bring from Norway?
Why have you traveled all alone,
in such great haste to see me?"

Hedin said:
"I have done an evil deed—
I swore on the toasting-cup a solemn oath
that the noble Svava, your bride, would be mine."

Helgi said:
"You've done nothing wrong; we may well desire,
both of us, that your oath be true:
a king has summoned me to come to the holm
three days from now and fight a duel.
I don't believe I can win that battle—
then what was fated will be best fulfilled."

. . . when he met a troll-woman. The troll-woman was Helgi's *fylgja,* a female guardian spirit whose appearance foretold his death.
the holm. An island dueling-place.

Hedin said:
"Helgi, you find   no fault with Hedin,
give him your heart   and grant him gifts.
Better to stain   your sword with blood
than offer friendship   to your foes!"

Helgi spoke as he did because he believed he would soon die and that it was his guardian-spirit that Hedin had seen in the form of a troll-woman riding a wolf.

Alf was the name of the king, Hrodmar's son, who had challenged Helgi to meet him three days later at Sigar's Field.

Then Helgi said:
"You met a woman   riding a wolf
at nightfall; she wanted   to follow you.
She knew   that Sigrlinn's son
would soon be slain   at Sigar's Field."

There was a great battle in which Helgi received his death-wound.

Helgi sent   Sigar to ride
after Eylimi's   only daughter,
and tell her not to linger   but leave at once
if she would come   to the king in time.

Sigar said:
"It is Helgi   who sends me here
with something to say   to you, Svava, only;
the warrior wants   to see you once again
before he breathes   his life's last breath."

Svava said:
"What's happened to Helgi,   Hjorvard's son?
You summon me   to heavy sorrow;

if the sea drowned him,   if a sword stabbed him,
I'll know what to do   to avenge his death."

Sigar said:
"He fell this morning   at Freka Stone,
the best of princes   beneath the sky;
Helgi's death   was the deed of Alf—
would that this day   had never dawned."

Helgi said:
"Hail to you, Svava!   Yield not to sorrow;
we two will meet   no more in this world.
Now the blood   wells from my breast;
close to my heart   the keen blade struck.

"I beg you, Svava,   my bride, don't weep!
Listen well,   and heed my words:
let my brother   share your bed,
to the young lord   turn now in love."

Svava said:
"I made a vow   in Munarheim
when Helgi gave me   golden rings:
I would not consent,   though the king be dead,
to hold another   in my arms."

Hedin said:
"Kiss me, Svava!   I will not come back
to Rogheim   or to Rodulsfells
before avenging Helgi,   Hjorvard's son,
who was the best hero   under heaven."

"I'll know what to do." This line is logical only in regard to Helgi's death by stabbing; Svava may be frenzied, or may refer to something we do not understand.

would that this day. . . . Literally, "though this time was not needed at all."

I will not come back. One has the impression that the poem breaks off at the beginning of a long story.

It is said of Helgi and Svava that they were born again.

It is said. . . . Professor Dunn suggests that the statement at the end of the poem may be a belated scribal attempt to link the old Helgi tradition to the Volsung-Helgi tradition.

THE SECOND LAY OF HELGI HUNDING'S BANE

Essentially the same material as The First Lay of Helgi, *but with a greatly heightened poetic quality. In this version Helgi is killed by Sigrun's brother Dag, and Helgi's last conversation with Sigrun takes place inside the grave-mound after his death.*

About the Volsungs

King Sigmund, the son of Volsung, married Borghild from Bralund. They called their son Helgi, for Helgi Hjorvard's son. Hagal was Helgi's foster-father.

There was a mighty king called Hunding. Hundland is named for him. He was a great warrior and had many sons who went out raiding. There was hatred and hostility between King Hunding and King Sigmund; each killed kinsmen of the other. King Sigmund and the men of his race were called Volsungs and Ylfings.

Helgi went in secret to spy on King Hunding's court. Haeming, one of Hunding's sons, was at home. When Helgi was leaving he met a shepherd and said:

"Tell Haeming   that Helgi remembers
a mail-clad warrior,   slayer of men;
you had a grey wolf   inside your hall,
and King Hunding   thought he was Hamal."

Hamal was the name of Hagal's son. King Hunding sent men to Hagal, looking for Helgi. There was no way out except for Helgi to disguise himself as a bondmaid and turn the grindstone. They searched and didn't find him.

Then Blind spoke   baleful words:
"Hagal's bondmaid   has piercing eyes—

---

remembers/a mail-clad warrior. Probably his own father, Sigmund.

a grey wolf. Ylf: "wolf"; hence, a Volsung or Ylfing.

Then Blind spoke. . . . This line is included in the stanza by Boer, but is printed as prose by Neckel.

I'd say a man   stands at the mill;
he grinds so hard   the stones are splitting.

"A bitter fate   follows the prince—
behold the chieftain   grinding barley!
It seems to me   those hands should hold
the haft of a sword,   not turn a mill."

Hagal answered him, saying:
"The millwheel's music   is no great marvel—
a king's daughter   stands at the quern;
once she strode   across the clouds,
and killed many men   with a Viking's courage.
Now she's here   as Helgi's captive.
She is a sister   of Hogni and Sigar:
Ylfing maidens   have fiery eyes."

Helgi got away and sailed in a warship. He killed King
Hunding and was afterwards called Helgi Hunding's Bane.
He landed in Bruna Bay, and raided the coast with his men;
they found cattle and ate the meat raw.

King Hogni had a daughter called Sigrun. She was a valkyrie
and rode through the sky and over the sea. She was Svava reborn. Sigrun rode to meet Helgi and said:

"Who brings the swift ships   to these shores?
Tell me, warriors,   where is your home?
What do you want   in Bruna Bay?
Where do you hope   to go from here?"

Helgi said:
"Hamal brings the swift ships   to these shores;
we have our homes   in the Isles of Hle.
Now we are waiting   for a fair wind
to bear us eastward   from Bruna Bay."

Sigrun said:
"Prince, where have you been   waging war,

feeding the geese   of Gunn's sisters?
Why is your byrnie   stained with blood,
why do men in armor   eat raw meat?"

Helgi said:
"Before he came here,   the son of kings
was in the Western Isles,   if you wish to know,
capturing bears   in Bragalund,
sating the eagles   with his spear.
Now I've told you, maiden,   why our meat was raw:
there isn't much steak   far out at sea."

Sigrun said:
"You speak of the battle   when Helgi's sword
felled King Hunding   dead on the field;
that great combat   avenged your kinsmen—
bright blood   streamed down your blade."

Helgi said:
"Noble lady,   how do you know,
wise as you are,   that we're those warriors?
Many are the proud   sons of princes,
keen men,   akin to us."

Sigrun said:
"I stood close by,   prince, when your sword
struck down that warrior   yesterday morning,
but I count it clever   of Sigmund's son
to speak in runes   that conceal his name.

"I've seen you before—   you were on a ship;
boldly you stood   on a bloodstained prow
while icy waves   played wildly about you.
Now the king hopes   to keep his secret,
but Hogni's daughter   knows Helgi well."

---

the geese of Gunn's sisters: ravens or eagles.
the Western Isles: Britain.

There was a mighty king named Granmar who lived at Svarin's Cairn. He had many sons: one was named Hodbrodd, another Gudmund, a third Starkad. Hodbrodd was at a meeting of kings and was promised the hand of Sigrun, Hogni's daughter. But when she heard about it, she rode with the valkyries through the air and over the sea to find Helgi.

Helgi was at Logafells where he fought against Hunding's sons, killing Alf and Eyjolf, Hjorvard and Hervard. Exhausted from the battle, he was sitting beneath Eagle Rock. There Sigrun found him. She threw her arms around his neck, kissed him, and told him the tidings, as it is related in *The Old Lay of the Volsungs:*

Sigrun came,   seeking the prince;
when she found Helgi   she took his hand,
kissed and greeted   the mail-clad warrior.
Then to her only   turned Helgi's heart.

Hogni's daughter   held nothing back,
asking Helgi   for his affection;
before she had ever seen   Sigmund's son,
she had loved him   with all her heart.

"All the host heard me   promised to Hodbrodd,
but I pledged myself   to another prince;
though I fear   my kinsmen's fury,
my father shall not   have his heart's desire."

Helgi said:
"Pay no heed   to Hogni's wrath,
or to your kinsmen's   cruel hearts!
From now on, maiden,   you shall be mine,
and none of your family   do I fear."

Hogni's daughter. This line and the one that follows are Neckel's stanza 16, printed here as in Boer.

Helgi assembled many warships and sailed to Freka Stone. At sea they were in great danger from a violent gale. Lightning flashed from above, striking the ships. Then they saw nine valkyries riding through the sky; one of them was Sigrun. The storm abated, and the ships came safely to land.

Granmar's sons were sitting on a cliff when the ships turned toward shore. Gudmund leaped onto his horse, and rode to look out from a hillside near the harbor. The Volsungs were just lowering their sails. Then Gudmund said, as it is written above in *The Lay of Helgi:*

"What king is steering   these mighty ships,
whose gold war-banner   waves on the prow?
No sign of peace   it seems to me,
that fiery glow   in front of the Vikings."

Sinfjotli, Sigmund's son, answered:
"Let Hodbrodd know   he'll find Helgi here,
the fearless warrior,   with his great fleet;
he has captured   your kinsmen's treasure,
he is heir   to the Fjorsung hoard."

Gudmund said:
"Let us first   at Freka Stone
meet in combat   to judge the case.
Hodbrodd, it's time   to take revenge—
too long we've been   the Volsungs' victims!"

Sinfjotli said:
"More likely, Gudmund,   you'll tend the goats
and climb about   on craggy cliffs;
you'll hold in your hands   a hazel club—
that will suit you better   than wielding a sword."

"What king is steering. . . ." The repetitive quotation preceding stanza 24 has been omitted.

Helgi said:
"Sinfjotli, it would be   much more fitting
to fight with men   and feed the eagles.
What's the use   of insulting words
even when ring-breakers   burn with rage!

"I expect no good   from Granmar's sons,
but worthy chieftains   won't twist the truth:
at Moinsheim   they made it clear
with what spirit   they use their swords.
They are warriors,   worthy foes."

Gudmund rode home with the news of war. Then Granmar's sons summoned the host. Many kings assembled. There was Hogni, Sigrun's father, and his sons Bragi and Dag. In a great battle all of Granmar's sons fell, and all the chieftains except Hogni's son Dag, who was given quarter and swore oaths to the Volsungs.

Sigrun went into the field and found Hodbrodd dying. She said:
"You won't have Sigrun   of Sefafells,
Hodbrodd, king,   to hold in your arms;
time has run out—   grey wolves sink their teeth
in slain men's bodies—   for Granmar's sons."

She found Helgi and was joyful. He said:
"Sigrun, I will grieve you   by what I say,
but evil Norns   must bear the blame:
there fell this morning   at Freka Stone
Bragi and Hogni;   I was their bane.

And at Hlefells   the sons of Hrollaug,
and King Starkad   at the Cliffs of Styr—
I found that warrior   fiercest of all:
his body fought on   with its head cut off.

"*Sinfjotli, it would be. . . .*" This stanza and the next are almost identical to stanzas 45 and 46 in *The First Lay of Helgi Hunding's Bane.*

Most of your family   has fallen here;
our swords have claimed   the lives of your kinsmen.
You couldn't stop the fight;   fate has made you
a cause of strife   among strong men."

Then Sigrun wept. He said:
"Take comfort, Sigrun!   You have been our shield-maid;
    nothing frees us from fate."

She said:
"Now I would wish   those warriors alive,
    and still have your arms around me."

Helgi and Sigrun married and had sons. Helgi didn't live to grow old. Dag, Hogni's son, sacrificed to Odin in order to have help in avenging his father. Odin lent Dag his spear. Dag met Helgi, his sister's husband, at a place called Fjoturlund. He ran Helgi through with his spear. There Helgi died. Dag rode to Sefafells and told Sigrun what had happened:

"Sister, I am sorry   for what I have to say—
I never wanted   to make you weep;
there fell this morning   at Fjoturlund
the best of warriors   in all the world,
who set his foot   on the neck of kings."

Sigrun said:
"Now all the oaths   you offered Helgi
shall be your doom   and strike you down,
vows you swore   by the shining Leiptr,
witnessed by Unn's   cold wet stone.

"The ship that carries you   shall not sail
though it be followed   by the fairest winds;
the horse you ride   shall refuse to run

Unn's cold wet stone. An altar, cold and wet from being near the sea.

though you have to flee   a foe's fury.
The blade you wield   shall never bite
until you hear it   close to your head.

"I would have vengeance   for Helgi's death
if you were a wolf   out in the woods;
denied all wealth   and all delight,
you'd leap on dead flesh   or long for food."

Dag said:
"Sister, you are mad,   out of your senses,
to hope your brother   finds such a fate!
Odin alone   has worked this evil:
he carried runes of strife   among close kin.

"I want to give you   golden rings,
Vandil's land,   the dales of Vig;
I say that you   and your sons shall hold
half our lands   to repay your loss."

Sigrun said:
"I'll live with sorrow   at Sefafells,
never again   will I know joy
unless a light breaks   over these lands
as gold-bitted Warwind   gallops with the host,
and I can welcome   the warrior home.

"Helgi struck terror   to the hearts
of all his foes,   their friends and kinsmen;
they fled before him,   as goats on the fells
run wildly   when they see a wolf.

"Helgi looked down   on other lords
as an ash tree stands   above a thorn,

as an ash tree stands. . . . The tone and imagery here are those of Gudrun mourning Sigurd. But Gudrun never spoke as fiercely as Sigrun later does (stanza 43).

or like the deer calf   shining with dew
who towers over   other beasts,
his bright horns raised   even to heaven."

A burial mound was raised over Helgi. And when he came to Valhalla, Odin let Helgi's judgment prevail equally with his own.

[Helgi said:
"Hunding, you must wait on   all the warriors,
washing their feet;   then light the fires,
tie up the hounds   and tend the horses,
give the swine their swill   before you sleep."]

One of Sigrun's bondwomen was near Helgi's grave one evening and saw Helgi riding toward the barrow with many men. The bondmaid said:

"Is it a dream   or the end of the world—
do I really see   dead men riding?
Will you spur   your steeds on further,
or have the heroes   come home to stay?"

Helgi said:
"What your eyes see   is not a dream,
nor does it mean   that the world is doomed,
although you see us   spurring our steeds;
nor have the heroes   come home to stay."

The bondmaid went home and said to Sigrun:
"Make haste, Sigrun   of Sefafells,
if you want   to look on your lord!
The barrow is open—   Helgi has come back;
the warrior bids you   tend his gaping wounds,
bind them up,   and stop their bleeding."

"Hunding, you must. . . ." It seems most likely that this stanza comes from another poem. The present Helgi would not have been so boorish.
nor have the heroes. That is, the heroes can come home only for the one visit.

Sigrun went into the barrow and said to Helgi:
"I am so hungry   to be with you again
I feel like Odin's hawks   when they want food
and find warm bodies   of warriors slain,
or see day's first light,   sparkling with dew.

"Let me kiss   the lifeless king
while you still wear   your bloodstained byrnie!
Heavy with frost   is Helgi's hair,
over his face   red rain has fallen,
icy and wet   are my husband's hands—
what can I do, prince,   to ease your pain?"

Helgi said:
"You alone, Sigrun   of Sefafells,
steep Helgi's shroud   in the dew of sorrow.
My sun-bright lady,   the bitter tears
you shed each night   before you go to sleep
are drops of blood   falling on my breast,
cold as rain, heavy   with your heart's grief.

"We'll fill our cups   with costly wine,
though lost forever   are life and lands.
Let no man utter   mournful dirges,
though my breast lies open   from a mortal blow;
for now my bride   has come to the barrow,
now a shield-maid   comforts the slain."

Sigrun arranged a bed in the grave-mound.
"Here in the barrow   we'll go to bed,
released from sorrow,   my royal lord.
I will sleep, Helgi,   safe in your arms
the way I used to   when you were alive."

Helgi said:
"Now I know   that nothing again

red rain has fallen. Literally, "the dew of sorrow," blood.

will seem a wonder   in Sefafells,
since you can sleep   in a dead man's arms,
white Sigrun, here   in Helgi's grave,
and you aren't dead,   O king's daughter!

"It's time I rode   the reddening ways,
spurring my pale horse   up the steep paths;
I must be beyond   the Rainbow Bridge
before Salgofnir   summons the host."

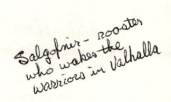

Salgofnir – rooster
who wakes the
warriors in Valhalla

Helgi and his men rode away, and Sigrun went home with her
women. The next evening Sigrun had a bondmaid keep watch
at the grave. At nightfall Sigrun came to the barrow and said:

"He would be here now   if he meant to come,
Sigmund's son Helgi,   from Odin's hall;
now it is nightfall   my hopes grow grey,
the eagles have gone   to roost on ash-trees
and people hasten   to the halls of dream."

The bondmaid said:
"Lady, you'd be mad   to linger alone
here where ghosts   live in their graves;
when the sun sets   their strength increases,
baleful are the dead   until the dawn."

Grief and sorrow caused Sigrun to die young.

In olden times it was believed that people could be born again,
although that is now considered an old woman's tale. Helgi and
Sigrun are said to have been reborn. He was then called Helgi
Hadding's Bane, and she Kara, daughter of Halfdane, as it is
told in *The Lay of Kara,* and she was a valkyrie.

The Lay of Kara. Apparently this poem has been lost.

THE PROPHECY OF GRIPIR

The story of Sigurd and Brynhild, plainly told.

Gripir was the name of Eylimi's son, the brother of Hjordis. This king was the wisest of men and the greatest seer. One day Sigurd, riding alone, came to Gripir's hall. A man named Geitir was standing outside. Sigurd, who was easy to recognize, spoke to him and asked:

"Who lives here in these strong halls?
What do the people call their king?"
Geitir said:
"Gripir is the name of our great prince,
a mighty lord of land and men."

Sigurd said:
"Is the wise ruler here at home?
will that warrior speak with me?
A friendless traveler needs to talk;
gladly would I see Gripir soon."

Geitir said:
"What answer shall Geitir give the king?
He will want to know the stranger's name."
Sigurd said:
"I am Sigurd, Sigmund's son,
and my mother's name is Hjordis."

Then to Gripir Geitir said:
"A stranger stands outside your door
who has the look of a noble lord;
he desires to speak with you."

The lord of warriors left the hall,
happy to greet the chieftain as a guest:

"Sigurd, I'm glad   to see you here at last!
You, Geitir,   take care of Grani!"

Then they talked   of many things,
the two warriors,   wise in counsel.

Sigurd said:
"Tell me, uncle,   if you see the truth,
what has life   in store for Sigurd?"

Gripir said:
"The mightiest of men   under the sun,
the noblest in birth   shall Sigurd be,
with gold free-handed,   fearless in a fight,
wonderful to look at,   wise in words."

Sigurd said:
"I would ask you more;   tell me, honest king,
all that your wisdom   lets you see.
What is fated   that I do first—
what will happen   when I leave your hall?"

Gripir said:
"You will first   avenge your father,
prince, and mine;   get payment for grief.
Soon the valiant   sons of Hunding
will have fallen   to your swift sword."

Sigurd said:
"Tell me, kinsman,   worthy king,
as we talk here   with open hearts,
do you see for Sigurd   such great deeds
as those which are highest   under the heavens?"

Gripir said:
"You will destroy   the gleaming dragon
that greedy lies   in Gnitaheath;

you alone will be   the bane of both
Regin and Fafnir.   Gripir is not wrong.''

Sigurd said:
"Wealth in abundance   I shall win,
and fame, if I fight   as you foresee;
look into your mind   and tell me more:
where is my life   to lead me next?''

Gripir said:
"You will find   the lair of Fafnir,
and gather up   his gleaming treasure,
Grani's back   you'll load with gold,
and ride to Gjuki,   the gallant lord.''

Sigurd said:
"More would I hear   from your heart,
bravest of princes.   Prophesy!
I'll be Gjuki's guest,   but when I go
what has life   in store for Sigurd?''

Gripir said:
"A prince's daughter   has lain asleep,
armed, on a hilltop,   since Helgi died.
You will seize   a sharp sword,
and cut her byrnie   with Fafnir's bane.''

Sigurd said:
"The armor broken,   the maiden awakes
out of her sleep,   and begins to speak;
what in her wisdom   will she say
that is to further   Sigurd's fortunes?''

Gripir said:
"She will reveal   the secret runes,

---

since Helgi died. The reference is obscure. It may identify him with Hjalgunnar,
the warrior Brynhild protected against Odin's will; or it may be simply an error.

the lore that all men   long to know,
teach you to speak   in every tongue
the words of healing.   Long life to the king!"

Sigurd said:
"Now with my learning   I shall leave
to ride again   along my road.
Look into your mind   once more and say
where my life   will lead me then."

Gripir said:
"You will come   to the house of a king,
glad to be there   as Heimir's guest.
I have told you, Sigurd,   all I can see;
do not ask me   to tell you more."

Sigurd said:
"I am saddened   by what you say.
You see further   into the future,
Gripir—you know   of grief for Sigurd,
and so you mean   to say no more."

Gripir said:
"Something of your youth   I could see
plainly enough   to prophesy;
I can speak no words   of true wisdom
or see into time;   what I know I've told."

Sigurd said:
"Gripir, no man   above the ground
sees into the future   further than you.
You shall not hide this,   though it be hateful,
even if you speak it   to my shame."

Gripir said:
"No fault lies   upon your life—
that I can promise,   illustrious prince!

As long as the world lasts   this will live,
a summons to battle: Sigurd's name."

Sigurd said:
"What could be worse   than that we part,
one from the other,   the way things are?
Let me hear   even what is hateful—
all of life   is laid down before!"

Gripir said:
"Now, Sigurd,   you'll hear me say
what is fated,   since I am forced;
all I tell you   will be true:
I know the day   that you must die."

Sigurd said:
"Great king, my uncle,   don't be angry,
but I wish to hear   more of your wisdom;
however vile the truth is,   tell me now—
what waits for Sigurd   on his way?"

Gripir said:
"When you are with Heimir,   in his house
you will find   a fair woman;
she is called Brynhild,   Budli's daughter,
Heimir fosters   the hard-minded maid."

Sigurd said:
"What will it matter   if a maiden
fostered by Heimir   is fair to see?
You can explain   more clearly, Gripir,
with all my life   laid out before you."

Gripir said:
"You will be deprived   of all delight
by the fair woman   Heimir fosters;

you will be robbed   of sleep and rest,
care for nothing more   except that maiden."

Sigurd said:
"What shall be solace   then for Sigurd?
Tell me, Gripir,   if you see the truth;
will I agree   to pay the bride-price
of Brynhild the fair,   Budli's daughter?"

Gripir said:
"The strongest oaths   you two will swear,
but few of your vows   will you fulfill;
when you have been Gjuki's   guest one night,
you will forget   Heimir's foster-daughter."

Sigurd said:
"Is this the fate   you see before me?
Will I, a king,   not be constant?
Will I break   my word to Brynhild
when I loved her   with all my heart?"

Gripir said:
"You will come   by evil counsel,
Grimhild's treachery,   to your grief:
she will give you   Gudrun, her daughter;
the bright-haired maiden   will be your bride."

Sigurd said:
"Worthy kinsmen   I will win
if I marry Gudrun,   Gunnar's sister;
I would have reason   then to rejoice,
unless that wedding   means my woe."

Gripir said:
"Grimhild will work   her wiles on you;
she'll want Brynhild   to be the bride

of Gunnar, her son,   the Gothic king.
Gladly you'll promise   to go and win her."

Sigurd said:
"Now I can see   the sorrow before me;
Sigurd's life   has fallen low
if the glorious maiden   I loved most
I win to be   another's bride."

Gripir said:
"Solemn oaths   you three will swear
to that—Sigurd,   Gunnar, and Hogni.
Then, as you travel,   you will be transformed
to look like Gunnar.   Gripir does not lie."

Sigurd said:
"What do you mean?   Why will we exchange
form and features?   It must mean
that foul deceit   will surely follow
if we travel so—   but tell me, Gripir."

Gripir said:
"You'll have Gunnar's face   and Gunnar's voice,
but keep your own   words and wisdom;
thus to Brynhild   you will be betrothed,
for Gunnar you'll win   the warrior-maid."

Sigurd said:
"Now I've heard the worst!   Worthy men
will have the right   to call me wicked!
I have no wish   to win by guile,
for Gunnar, a bride,   the best of women."

the Gothic king. "Gothic," here, is used imprecisely.

to go and win her. The poet is attempting to merge various versions of Sigurd's misadventures by having Sigurd visit Gjuki twice, once before meeting Brynhild and once after. The valkyrie is not identified as Brynhild.

Gripir said:
"Lord of warriors,   you will lie in bed
with that maiden,   as if she were your mother;
so will Sigurd's   name stand high
as long as the world   lives to remember."

Sigurd said:
"Tell me, Gripir,   will Gunnar still
take that woman   for his wife,
knowing I had near me   for three nights
his quick-minded bride?   I can't believe it!"

Gripir said:
"Together you will drink   at the double wedding
of Sigurd and Gunnar   in Gjuki's hall;
you will have returned then   to your real forms;
each of you had always   his own mind."

Sigurd said:
"What will happen after?   Will we be happy
to have so married?   Tell me, Gripir!
Will Gunnar live   long in delight
with his wife,   and I with mine?"

Gripir said:
"You will remember   the oaths you swore,
yet keep silent   and live with Gudrun;
but Brynhild, unhappy   with her husband,
will vow to work   her own revenge."

Sigurd said:
"How will Brynhild   avenge her wrongs,
the bride whom we   have so betrayed?
She has, from Sigurd,   solemn oaths,
none fulfilled,   and little joy."

Gripir said:
"She will give her husband,   Gjuki's heir,
reason to think   that he was wronged,
tricked that time   when Gunnar trusted
the warrior pledged   to win his bride."

Sigurd said:
"Is this the fate   that you foresee?
Will what she tells Gunnar   be the truth?
Or will that lord   believe a lie
he hears from Brynhild   about herself and me?"

Gripir said:
"In her rage   and heavy sorrow
she'll turn against you   to take revenge;
but to her   you did no harm
although your guile   won Gunnar his wife."

Sigurd said:
"Will the wise Gunnar   do her will,
and Guthorm and Hogni   also agree?
Tell me, Gripir,   will Gjuki's sons
redden their swords   with Sigurd's blood?"

Gripir said:
"Grief will harrow   Gudrun's heart;
her brothers will decide   that you shall die.
Joy will leave   her life forever—
for all this, Grimhild   bears the guilt.

"Let this at least   console you, Sigurd:
you will be fortunate   in your fame;
in all the world   no man more worthy
ever will be seen   beneath the sky."

Sigurd said:
"Uncle, farewell!   No one conquers fate.
You have done all   that I desired.
You would have been glad   to say good things
of what is coming,   if you could."

THE LAY OF REGIN

Regin explains to his foster-son Sigurd how Fafnir unjustly acquired that gold which would ultimately become the Niflung hoard. Before attempting to kill Fafnir, Sigurd sets out to avenge his father, Sigmund, and meets Odin who gives him advice.

Sigurd went to Hjalprek's herd, and chose for himself a horse which was afterwards called Grani. At that time Regin, Hreidmar's son, was visiting Hjalprek. He was the cleverest of craftsmen, a dwarf in stature; he was wise and cruel, and skilled in magic. Regin was Sigurd's foster-father; he taught him, and loved him very much. He told Sigurd about his own ancestors, and how it happened once that Odin and Hoenir and Loki came to Andvari's Falls, in which there were many fish. A dwarf named Andvari had lived for a long time in the waterfall in the shape of a pike and got food for himself there. "We had a brother called Otter," said Regin, "who often came to the waterfall in the shape of an otter. He had caught a salmon, and sat dozing on the river bank while he ate it. Loki threw a stone at him and killed him. The gods thought this very good luck, and skinned the otter. That same evening they asked Hreidmar for hospitality overnight, and showed their catch. Then we seized them and set this as their ransom: they must fill the otterskin, and cover it outside too, with gold. They sent Loki to find the gold. He went to Ran and asked for her net. Then he went to Andvari's Falls and cast the net in front of the pike; and it leaped into the net. Then Loki said:

"What kind of fish   can swim the falls
    but fails to ward off woe?
If you want to keep   your head out of Hel,
    find me what flames in water."

Sigurd went to Hjalprek's herd. After Sigmund's death, Hjordis married King Hjalprek's son, and Sigurd grew up at his court.
what flames in water: gold.

The pike said:
"My name is Andvari,   Odin is my father;
    many falls I've followed.
Long ago a foul Norn   fixed as my fate
    to spend my life swimming."

Loki said:
"Tell me this, Andvari,   unless you think
    you've lived too long on Earth:
what is the penalty   men must pay
    who fight their wars with words?"

Andvari said:
"Much will they suffer,   the sons of men
    who wade in Vadgelmir's waters;
one who speaks   false words to another
    will walk there long."

Andvari showed Loki his gold. When it had all been handed over, Andvari still had a ring, and Loki took it from him. The dwarf went into a cave and said:

"Now the gold   that belonged to Gust
shall bring two brothers   to their bane,
and drive eight princes   to discord and death;
by my wealth   no man wins pleasure."

The Aesir delivered the gold to Hreidmar; they filled the otter skin and stood it on its feet. Then they had to pile up enough gold to cover it. When that was done, Hreidmar came forward and, seeing one whisker, told the Aesir to cover it. Then Odin hid the hair with Andvari's ring.

Loki said:
"We've paid the ransom;   you have received
    the high price set on my head.

Gust: otherwise unidentified.

But to your son   it will seem no blessing;
   the gold is a bane to you both."

Hreidmar said:
"I see how gladly   you gave those gifts—
   with hatred in your hearts.
The Aesir lords   would have lost their lives
   had I foreseen our fate."

Loki said:
"Worse yet,   my wisdom tells me,
   will be the clash of kinsmen;
by the gold's power,   princes not yet born
   will turn their hearts to hate."

Hreidmar said:
"All that treasure   shall be mine alone
   until the day I die;
you will not find me   fearful of threats—
   now all you gods, go home!"

Fafnir and Regin asked Hreidmar for a share of their brother's wergild. Hreidmar refused. Then Fafnir struck his father with a sword while Hreidmar was sleeping. Hreidmar called to his daughters:

"Lyngheid, Lofnheid,   life is leaving me!
   Now I will need your help."

Lyngheid answered:
"A father may die,   but few sisters
   console themselves killing a brother."

---

by the gold's power. . . . Future princes will covet the gold and destroy each other to have it.

Now I will need your help. Hreidmar is asking his daughter to avenge his death.

Hreidmar said:
"You would do well,   my wolf-hearted daughter,
if by your husband   you have no sons,
to give him a girl-child;   in your great need,
her son   will avenge your sorrow."

Then Hreidmar died. Fafnir took all the gold. Regin asked for his share, but Fafnir wouldn't give him anything. Then Regin took counsel with Lyngheid as to how he should get his inheritance back. She said:

"Go in friendship   and ask that Fafnir
   give you both gold and good will;
you would be wrong   to reach for a sword
   when you seek a brother's boon."

Regin told Sigurd all these things. One day when Sigurd came to Regin's house he was warmly welcomed. Regin said:

"Here we see   the son of Sigmund,
boldest of heroes,   in our own hall;
his wrath is mightier   than a grown man's.
When the wolf hungers,   I look for war.

"I will care   for the mighty king,
the royal chieftain   raise as my son;
nowhere on earth   is there his equal,
his lines of fate   overlie all lands."

From then on Sigurd was always with Regin, who told him that Fafnir lay on Gnitaheath in the shape of a serpent and had the Helm of Terror, which all living things feared. Regin made Sigurd a sword which was called Gram. It was so sharp

---

"You would do well." This seems to be a kind, if obscure, bit of prophetic advice. Apparently Hreidmar is not angered by Lyngheid's refusal, unless he is speaking ironically. The stanza may be out of place.

the royal chieftain. Yngir's son, descendent of kings.

that when he thrust it into the Rhine and floated a tuft of wool downstream against it, the blade cut through the wool as if it were water. With this sword Sigurd cut Regin's anvil in two. After that Regin urged Sigurd to kill Fafnir. Sigurd said:

"I'd hear loud laughter   from Hunding's sons
by whose hands Eylimi   lost his life,
if Sigmund's son   would rather seek
red-gold rings   than avenge his father."

King Hjalprek helped Sigurd seek vengeance by giving him a manned ship. Meeting a great storm, he sailed close to a certain rocky point of land. A man stood on the cliff and said:

"Who rides there   on Raevil's horse
over steep crests   of crashing seas?
Stained white   with salty sweat,
how will your wave-steeds   weather the wind?"

Regin answered:
"Sigurd and his men,   high on the sea-trees,
follow a fair wind   straight to Hel;
huge breakers plunging   over the prow
stampede the wave-steeds—   who wants to know?"

The man said:
"My name was Hnikar   when the raven rejoiced,
young Sigurd,   to see my prey.
Now you may call   the man from the cliff
Feng or Fjolnir,   and let me fare with you."

They steered toward land, and as soon as the man came aboard the ship the storm abated.

---

by whose hands Eylimi. . . . Eylimi and his son-in-law Sigmund were killed in the same battle against Hunding's sons.

Sigurd said:
"Tell me, Hnikar—   you must know
  omens for gods and for men,
which are the best   when there's a battle,
  what signs when swords are sweeping?"

Hnikar said:
"Many things are good,   if men but know
  the signs when swords are sweeping;
those dark spots, ravens,   seen in the sky
  are faithful friends to the warrior.

"This is a second: when you start out
  ready for the road,
if you see   standing in your path
  two praiseworthy warriors.

"This is a third: if you hear a wolf
  howling from a wood,
you're sure to win   when you meet warriors
  whose faces you don't see first.

"A man is foolish   if he fights
where the setting sun   can strike his eyes;
no one wins battles   half blind
against brave warriors   in wedge-shaped columns.

"It's a bad sign   if you should stumble
  as you go forth to fight;
deceitful spirits   standing at your side
  desire to see you down.

"Morning sees the wise man   washed and combed,
  having eaten his fill of food;

Sigurd said. . . . Stanzas 19 through 25 must be an interpolation.
deceitful spirits. In the original, it is specified that these spirits are female.

you never know   what nightfall will bring:
   don't forego good fortune.''

Sigurd had a great battle with Lyngvi, Hunding's son, and his
brothers. There Lyngvi fell, and his three brothers with him.
After the battle Regin said:

"A sharp-biting sword   cut the blood-eagle
out of the back   of Sigmund's bane!
When was a warrior   worthier than he
who dyed the earth red   and rejoiced the raven?"

the blood-eagle. A method of putting to death, specific for the slayer of one's
father if taken alive in a battle. The ribs are cut in the shape of an eagle, and the
lungs pulled through the opening (Cleasby-Vigfusson).

THE LAY OF FAFNIR

Sigurd and Fafnir have a conversation before the dragon dies. Sigurd kills Regin, following the advice of birds who then direct him to Fafnir's gold and the valkyrie asleep on a fire-encircled mountain.

Sigurd went home to Hjalprek. Then Regin goaded him to kill Fafnir. Sigurd and Regin went up to Gnitaheath and followed the trail along which Fafnir slithered toward the water. Then Sigurd dug a great ditch in the path, and got into it. When Fafnir crawled away from his hoard, venom spurted from his mouth and flowed from above onto Sigurd's head. When Fafnir passed over the pit, Sigurd drove his sword into the serpent's heart. Fafnir thrashed about, striking his head and tail on the ground. Sigurd leaped out of the pit, and they confronted each other. Fafnir said:

"A boy, just a boy!   What mother gave you birth?
  Who says you are his son?
A bright blade is red   with Fafnir's blood;
  your sword stands in my heart."

Sigurd concealed his name because it was believed in ancient times that the words of a man about to die had great power if he cursed his enemy by name. He said:

"A wanderer named   for a noble beast,
  the son of no mother,
I had no father   as other men do;
  always I go alone."

Fafnir said:
"If you had no father   as other men do,
  what wonder begot you?"

---

named for a noble beast. Perhaps "man" (Boer).

Sigurd said:

"I tell you, my family   has no fame,
    any more than I myself;
I am called Sigurd,   my father Sigmund,
    and by my sword you were slain."

Fafnir said:

"Who drove you to it?   What made you decide
    to try to take my life?
I see how your eyes flash—   bold was the father
    whose son attacks unafraid."

Sigurd said:

"My heart drove me to it,   helped by my hand
    and the keen blade I carry;
few will be heroes   when their hair is white
    if childhood saw them craven."

Fafnir said:

"If you could have grown up   close to your kin,
    you would be bold in battle,
but you were caught   and kept in bonds;
    a man not free is afraid."

Sigurd said:

"You mock me, Fafnir,   because I'm far away
    from family and home;
maybe I was caught,   but I'm no captive—
    you felt my freedom to your cost."

Fafnir said:

"Words of hatred   are all you want to hear,
    but what I tell you is true:

my family has no fame. Sigurd continues to try to conceal his identity, although
he gives his name.
caught and kept in bonds. Sigurd was in fact brought up in Hjalprek's court, but
not as a captive.

the ringing gold,   the fire-red treasure
  will drag you down to your doom."

Sigurd said:
"Every warrior   enjoys his wealth
  until one destined day;
sooner or later   each man surrenders
  all that he has to Hel."

Fafnir said:
"You are destined   by the Norns' decree
  to find a fool's fate;
row in the wind   and you'll drown in water:
  all is danger to the doomed."

Sigurd said:
"Tell me, Fafnir,   famed for your wisdom—
  I know you've learned much lore,
what Norns will help   women in their need
  before they give birth?"

Fafnir said:
"The Norns descend   from different races,
  they have no common kin,
some from the gods,   some from the elves,
  some are Dvalin's daughters."

Sigurd said:
"Tell me, Fafnir,   famed for your wisdom—
  I know you've learned much lore,
what is the island   where blood will flow
  when gods and the fire-giant fight?"

Fafnir said:
"It's called Ill-Fated,   for the time to come
  when the gods will go to war;

"Tell me, Fafnir. . . ." Stanzas 12 through 15 seem to be interpolated (Boer).

the Rainbow Bridge   will break as they ride,
   their horses swim in the stream.

"The Helm of Terror   I held over men
   as I lay guarding the gold;
I found no one   I had to fear,
   few were worth a fight."

Sigurd said:
"Don't trust   your Helm of Terror
   when strong men meet in battle;
if he fights enough,   a warrior will find
   that no one's courage conquers all."

Fafnir said:
"I blew out poison   as I lay protecting
   my father's treasure."

Sigurd said:
"Yes, fiery serpent,   fiercely you hissed
   and held to your hoard;
but men meet their foes   with greater fury
   if they have that Helm."

Fafnir said:
"Listen to me, Sigurd,   and heed what I say—
   ride home from here in haste!
The fire-red treasure,   the ringing gold,
   my hoard will be your bane.

"Regin betrayed me,   he will betray you,
   my brother will destroy us both;
Fafnir must leave   his life behind,
   and you have proved your power."

"*Regin betrayed me.*" This and the next stanza are ordered according to Boer.

Sigurd said:
"You were betrayed,   but I'll make my own
    what's hidden in the heath,
while Fafnir lies here   and fights with death
    until Hel holds him!"

Regin kept out of the way while Sigurd was slaying Fafnir.
Sigurd was wiping the blood from his sword when Regin came
back and said:

"Hail to the hero!   Well have you won
    the fight with Fafnir!
Sigurd, of all men   under the sun,
    not one was born so brave."

Sigurd said:
"When war-gods meet   to match their might,
    who can tell the bravest born?
Many a hero   never made a hole
    in another man's breast."

Regin said:
"You are happy, Sigurd,   your heart is light
    as you dry Gram with grass;
but it's my brother   whose blood you shed,
    and I bear some of the blame."

Sigurd said:
"By your will only   I rode this way
    over the highlands here;
long would the serpent   lie on his hoard,
    but you dared me to the deed."

"You were betrayed" Boer's interpretation.

"When war-gods meet. . . ." The translation of this stanza combines two lines,
one repeated from stanza 23. Sigurd's subsequent remark about heroism seems
more probably mocking than modest.

Regin went to Fafnir and cut out his heart with the sword called Ridil, and then he drank from the wound. Regin said:

"Sit down now, Sigurd;   wait while I sleep,
   and roast Fafnir's heart in the fire!
I have a mind   to eat this meat
   since I swallowed this blood."

Sigurd said:
"You were far away   when Fafnir's blood
   reddened my sharp sword;
I set my strength   against the serpent
   while you hid in the heather."

Regin said:
"You would have let   the old giant lie
   for a long time yet in his lair
had not my skill   forged you your sword,
   that bright blade you carry."

Sigurd said:
"Spirit is better   than the keenest sword
   when there's a real foe to fight;
I've seen a brave man   swiftly win a battle
   though his blade was blunt.

"Courage is better   than cowardice
   for winning games of war;
gladness is always   better than gloom,
   whatever deeds must be done."

Sigurd took Fafnir's heart and roasted it on a spit. When he thought that it had cooked enough and the blood frothed out, he touched it to find out whether it was done. It burned him

the old giant. Although he was a dwarf in size, Regin, like Fafnir, was of the race of giants.
"Courage is better. . . ." Probably an interpolated stanza (Boer).

and he put his finger in his mouth. Then Fafnir's heartblood
touched his tongue, and he understood the speech of the birds.
He heard the nuthatches crying in the wood. One of them said:

"There sits Sigurd   stained with blood;
Fafnir's heart   he roasts in the fire.
I would call the prince   wise and prudent
if he himself   ate that gleaming heart."

Another said:
"There lies Regin   plotting revenge—
he wants to trick   the boy who trusts him.
The evil smith   speaks in crooked words,
blaming Sigurd   for his brother's death."

A third said:
"Cut off his head!   Send that hoary wizard
    straight down to Hel!
Why should Sigurd   share the treasure
    Fafnir left in his lair?"

A fourth said:
"He would understand   how to act wisely,
if he could have   your counsel, sisters,
to watch out for himself   and rejoice the raven—
I expect the wolf   when I see his ears."

A fifth said:
"He is not so wise,   this mighty warrior—
he doesn't look   like a war-lord to me
if he lets Regin   leave this place
when he has been   Fafnir's bane."

Another said. The number of birds involved is uncertain. Stanzas 34, 37, and 38
may well be uttered by the same violent voice.

The sixth said:
"He will be stupid   if he spares
   so foul a foe;
when Regin lies here   longing to destroy him—
   what makes Sigurd so blind!"

The seventh said:
"Shorter by a head   send the frost-hearted giant
   far from his red-gold rings!
Sigurd would have   the hoard of Fafnir,
   possess that prize all alone."

Sigurd said:
"Fate will not rule   that by Regin's hand
   I lose my life;
very soon both   of the giant brothers
   will have left here for Hel."

Sigurd cut off Regin's head, and then he ate Fafnir's heart and drank the blood of both Regin and Fafnir. Then he heard the birds saying:

"Pack on your saddle   the red rings, Sigurd—
few things worry   a worthy king;
I can find you   the fairest of maidens,
much wealth you'll have   if you can win her.

"Green roads lead   to Gjuki's domain—
fortune stands behind   a man who's bold—
there the great ruler   rears a daughter;
he would give her   for Sigurd's gold.

"There is a hall   on Hindarfell
fenced around   by a wall of flame;

the fairest of maidens: Gudrun.

wise men built it   there on the mountain
out of bright gold   gleaned from rivers.

"There is a shield-maid   asleep on the mountain,
the bane of tinder   surrounds her bed;
Odin struck her   with a sleep-thorn:
she had slain warriors   he wanted to win.

"Sigurd! You can see   the warrior maiden
where Vingskornir bore her   out of the battle;
prince, you might summon   Sigrdrifa from sleep,
but that depends   on the Norns' decree."

Sigurd followed Fafnir's trail to his lair and found it open. The
doors and door-frames were of iron; iron also were all the
beams of the house which was set into the earth.

There Sigurd found a great amount of gold and filled two
chests with it. He took the Helm of Terror, the gold byrnie, the
sword Hrotti, and many treasures, and loaded them onto Grani.
But the horse would not move forward until Sigurd was on his
back too.

the bane of tinder: fire.
sleep-thorn: a primitive hypodermic.

After Sigurd has awakened the valkyrie, here called Sigrdrifa, she gives him advice in the style of Sayings *of the High One.*

Sigurd rode up to the top of Hindarfell and from there went south to the land of the Franks. He saw a great light on a mountain, as if a fire were burning there; the flames reached to the heavens. When he came close, he saw a shield-wall and on it a golden banner. Sigurd went through the shield-wall and saw a man lying there asleep in full armor. First he took off the warrior's helmet. Then he saw that it was a woman. Her byrnie was so tight it seemed to have grown into her flesh. He cut it with Gram, from the neckpiece all the way down and through both sleeves. When he took the byrnie off her, she awakened and sat up. She saw Sigurd and said:

"What broke the byrnie?   Who summons me from sleep?
   How was I saved   from the ghostly spells?"
He said:
"Sigmund's son   and Sigurd's sword,
which just gave the ravens   reason to rejoice."

She said:
"Long I slept,   long did I slumber
   long are woes in the world;
it's Odin's fault   that I found no way
   to break the slumber-spells.

"Hail to the day,   hail to the sons of day,
   hail to night and its daughter!
Gaze on us gently,   grant us sitting here
   your blessing on our battles.

"Hail to the gods,   hail to the goddesses,
   hail to the all-giving Earth!

gave the ravens reason to rejoice. That is, he had just killed Fafnir and Regin.

1–4

Wisdom and lore,   as long as we live,
  grant us, and healing hands!"

Sigurd sat down and asked her name.
She was called Sigrdrifa, and she was a valkyrie. She told him
that there had been a battle between two kings, and Odin had
promised the victory to Hjalm-Gunnar, who was old and the
greatest of warriors, but

Agnar was the other,   Auda's brother.
He had never asked   help from anyone.

Sigrdrifa felled Hjalm-Gunnar in the battle, but Odin pricked
her with a sleep-thorn in revenge for this and said that never
again would she be victorious in battle and that she would be
given in marriage. "But I told him that I solemnly vowed for my
part never to marry any man who knew what fear was."

Sigurd asked her to teach him wisdom if she had knowledge
of all the worlds. Then she took a horn full of mead and gave
him a drink which would make him remember.

Sigrdrifa said:
"First I will bring   beer to the warrior—
might brewed it,   mingled with it fame—
full of spells   and potent songs,
rich in charms   and runes of joy.

"I shall teach you   the runes of triumph
  to have on the hilt of your sword—
some on the blade,   some on the guard;
  then call twice on Tyr.

"Ale-runes you will want   if another man's wife
  tries to betray your trust;

Sigurd sat down. . . . the prose is inserted as in Boer.
the warrior. "The warrior" here translates "combat's apple tree."

scratch them on your drinking-horn,   the back of your hand,
   and the need-rune on your nail.

"With this sign your horn   can never harm you;
   dip a leek in your drink;
then I know   you will never find
   death mixed into your mead.

"I'll teach you lore for helping   women in labor,
   runes to release the child;
write them on your palms   and clasp her wrists
   invoking the disir's aid.

"I can show you runes   to calm the surf
   and bring sail-steeds to safety;
write them on the prow   and on the rudder,
   blaze them into the oar-blades.
No seas are so black,   no breakers so wild,
   but that you'll escape the storm.

"Here are the limb-runes   that heal the sick
   and close the worst of wounds;
write them on the bark   of a forest tree
   with eastward-bending branches.

"I'll give you speech-runes   so none will seek
   to do you harm out of hatred;
wind some,   weave some,
   twist them all together,
carry them with you   where men hold court
   and many meet at the Thing.

"Mind-runes will let you   surpass all men
   because your wits are wiser;

"I'll give you speech-runes." These would prevent a man's speaking in such a
way as to inspire hatred.

read some,   write some,
    they came from Odin's cries;
and you shall learn   the lore that leaked
    from Heiddraupnir's skull,
    from Hoddrofnir's horn.

"He stood on a mountain,   his sword unsheathed,
    with a helmet on his head.

    "Then Mimir's head spoke
    the first wise word,
    and told true runes.

"On the shield that stands   before the shining god,
on Arvakr's ear   and Alsvinn's hoof,
on a wheel revolving   under Hrungnir's chariot,
on Sleipnir's teeth,   on the straps of a sled,
on a bear's paw,   on Bragi's tongue,
on the claws of a wolf   and an eagle's beak,
on bloody wings   and a bridge's head,
on a midwife's hand,   on the footprints of help,
on glass, on gold,   on good-luck charms,
in wine, in wort,   on the wished-for chair,
on Gungnir's point   and Grani's breast,
the nail of a Norn,   a night-owl's beak.

"Whatever they were scratched on   they were scraped off
    and mixed with holy mead
    sent far and wide,
some to the Aesir,   some to the Elves,
    some to the Vanir,
    some to sons of men.

they came from Odin's cries. That is, they were the thoughts of Hropt, "Odin
the Crier."

"He stood on a mountain." "He" is Odin, but the connection between the two
stanzas is uncertain.

the wished-for chair. Literally, "the seat of joy."

"There are runes of beech-wood,   others help at births,
   and all the ale-runes,
   promises of power.
Whoever holds them   unbroken, unchanged,
   will have good luck
   and be glad of his lore
   until the day of doom.

"Now you must tell me   which to take,
   warrior, of two ways;
shall I speak further,   or keep silence?
   Nothing frees us from fate."

Sigurd said:
"I will not flee   though you foretell my death—
   I was never called a coward;
I would keep your friendship   and your counsel
   as long as I live."

Sigrdrifa said:
"This I say first: don't give your family
   reason to reproach you,
or be too ready   to seek revenge
   though the dead deserve it.

"Second, you must never   swear an oath
   if you can't be sure you'll keep it:
there's bitter reward   for broken vows,
   a grim fate for the faithless.

"Third, be careful   at the Thing
   to speak with men of sense:

"Now you must tell me." Here the valkyrie offers to foretell the future if Sigurd
wishes her to. The translation follows Boer's interpretation.

or be too ready. That is, don't be too excessive about seeking revenge, even
with cause. The last half of the stanza seems to apply also to the family, and
to suggest that even just vengeance should be avoided among relatives; but the
last line is conjectural.

by what he says,   a stupid man may do
    more harm than he knows.

"When you are accused,   if you keep silent
    they'll call you a coward
    or believe the lie.
    Don't trust your friends
    to defend your fame.
Later, cut off   the liar's life—
    that's his rightful reward!

"Fourth, if you find out   that an evil witch
    lives along your way,
don't stop   and ask for shelter
    though night be falling fast.

"A man must take care   and keep both eyes open
    when he goes forth to fight:
sometimes a wicked woman   waits by the road
    to blunt his wits and weapons.

"Fifth, in a hall   if you should find
    beautiful women on the benches,
let no gleam of silver   keep you from sleep;
    do not lure them to love!

"Sixth, when men   sit drinking ale,
    and the talk is turning hostile,
don't dispute   with drunken warriors—
    wine steals the wits of many.

"Ale and fighting words,   you'll often find,
    are sources of sorrow;

"When you are accused." This phrase is implied, rather than stated, in the text.
no gleam of silver. That is, presumably, dazzling attire.
fighting words. Boer's *sennur,* not *söngr.*

they lead to disaster   or to death—
   the world knows many woes.

"Seventh, I counsel you,   if you have cause
   to quarrel with men of courage,
it's better to fight them   before they set on fire
   your house with you inside it.

"Eighth, take care   that you do no evil,
   flee from all that is false;
don't tempt a maiden   or another man's wife
   with promises of pleasure.

"I tell you, ninth, to bury   bodies of the dead
   when you find them on your way,
killed by sickness,   drowned in the sea,
   or slain by weapons of war.

"You shall bathe   the dead man's body,
   wash his hands and head,
dry him, comb his hair,   place him in a coffin,
   tell him to sleep in peace.

"Tenth, I advise you   never to trust
   the word of a warrior
   if you're his brother's bane
   or you've felled his father.
In a young son see a wolf
   though gladly he takes your gold.

"Fighting words and hate   aren't easily forgotten
   or sorrow quickly soothed;
a warrior needs   both wit and weapons
   if he seeks to surpass other men.

You shall bathe. . . . This would seem to be a Christian addition.
A warrior. Vargdropi interpreted according to Boer.

"Eleventh, I would have you   watch out for evil
  that you may find among friends.
I think the prince's life   cannot last long:
  the bitter strife has begun."

Here a large section is lost from the manuscript tradition.

FRAGMENT OF A SIGURD LAY

All that remains of what must have been a particularly dramatic account of the Sigurd story.

"Why do you seek   to kill Sigurd,
what has the hero done   to make you hate him?"

Gunnar said:
"I had Sigurd's   sworn oaths,
oaths he swore,   and all of them false;
I was betrayed   when I believed
Sigurd would not break   a solemn oath."

Hogni said:
"You believed   what Brynhild said
to sharpen your hatred,   hoping to do harm;
she is jealous   of Gudrun's joy,
nor is she glad   that you share her bed."

A wolf was roasted,   a snake was sliced,
and portions given   Guthorm to eat,
before they accomplished   their evil desire
and laid hands   on the matchless hero.

Outside stood Gudrun,   Gjuki's daughter;
she said these words   when she saw her brothers:
"Where is Sigurd,   the lord of warriors?
Why have my kinsmen   come home without him?"

Only Hogni   gave her an answer:
"We've cut him to pieces   with our swords;
beside the dead hero   the grey horse droops his head."

"I had Sigurd's sworn oaths." Gunnar refers to Sigurd's promise not to touch Brynhild.

given Guthorm to eat. According to *The Short Lay of Sigurd,* Guthorm was outside the oaths, and so selected to do the killing. To persuade him, they prepared a magic meal.

Then said Brynhild,   Budli's daughter:
"Well may you enjoy   your lands and weapons;
Sigurd alone   would have held it all
if he had lived   a little longer.

"It would not be right   for him to rule
Gjuki's legacy   and all the Goths;
five sons of his,   eager for fighting,
could well lead   the hosts to war."

Brynhild laughed—   the whole hall resounded—
just once,   with all her heart:
"Long may you enjoy   your lands and thanes,
you who brought down   the bravest of men!"

Then said Gudrun,   Gjuki's daughter:
"Monstrous words   come from your mouth—
may devils take Gunnar   for Sigurd's death!
Your cruelty   shall cost you dear."

Sigurd was slain   south of the Rhine;
up in a tree   a raven cried:
"Atli's blade   will be red with blood,
when your lives pay   for broken pledges."

It was late in the evening,   much ale had been drunk,
no harsh words   were heard in the hall;
then they were sleepy   and went to bed,
but Gunnar lay awake   longer than the others.

Moving his feet   and muttering words,
the ravener of hosts   revealed his mind:
he remembered   the raven and the eagle
who cried from a tree   when they were coming home.

---

five sons of his. "His" may refer to Gjuki, who elsewhere is credited with only
three sons, or else to Sigurd himself, the five sons then being hypothetical.
the raven and the eagle. The latter is not mentioned above, in stanza 11.

Budli's daughter,   Brynhild, woke up,
the queenly woman,   before dawn came:
"Urge me on or hinder me,   the harm is done—
I'll tell my sorrow,   or die in silence!"

No one spoke   when she said these words;
they were unable   to understand
why she wept   as she spoke of deeds
which laughing she   had lured them to do.

"Gunnar, as I slept   I had a grim dream:
the hall was chill,   and cold my bed,
but you, prince, rode   deprived of cheer
among your foes,   and your feet were fettered.
Now I know   that the Niflung might,
oath-breakers,   will come to an end.

"Gunnar, you forgot   that once in friendship
your blood and Sigurd's   flowed together;
he has received   a poor reward
for wanting to make you   foremost of men.

"How can you doubt,   since he came riding
fearless through fire   to ask me in marriage,
that the host-destroyer   held above all
the solemn promise   he gave the young prince?

"The blade of his sword,   bright with gold,
lay between me   and that noble lord,
fire-hardened   when it was forged,
with drops of poison   placed inside."

THE LAY OF GUDRUN

*The gentlest and most beautiful of the poems which describe
Gudrun after Sigurd's death.*

Close to death   in her despair,
Gudrun sat grieving   over Sigurd.
She did not wail   or wring her hands,
nor did she weep   like other women.

Noblemen came   to give her comfort,
spoke wise words   to soothe her heart.
Yet Gudrun could not   give way to tears;
burdened by grief,   her heart would break.

Great ladies   decked in gold
sat with Gudrun;   each one spoke,
telling the sorrows   she had suffered,
the bitterest   each one had borne.

Gjuki's sister,   Gjaflaug, said:
"I think no woman   in the world
hapless as I am—five husbands,
three daughters,   three sisters,
eight brothers lost;   and I live on."

Yet Gudrun could not   give way to tears;
hating those   who had killed her husband,
she sat with Sigurd,   her heart like stone.

Then said Herborg,   queen of the Huns:
"I have greater   griefs to tell.
At war in the south,   my seven sons,
and then my husband—   all have been slain;
my father and mother,   my four brothers,
all, when the wind   whipped the waves,
were struck down   in their ship at sea.

"I alone laid them out,   I alone buried them,
I alone gave them   an honored grave.
All this I suffered   in just one season,
and no one came   to comfort me.

"Then I was caught   and held a captive
in that same season;   I was a slave.
Every day   I had to dress
my lord's lady,   and lace her shoes.

"Her jealous spite   spared me no threats,
and she would beat me   hard blows.
No house could boast   a better master,
nor have I met   a mistress worse."

Yet Gudrun could not   give way to tears;
hating those   who had killed her husband,
she sat with Sigurd,   her heart like stone.

Gjuki's daughter,   Gullrond, spoke:
"Foster-mother,   your wisdom fails you—
how shall a young wife   listen to words?"
She told them not to keep   the dead prince concealed.

She swept off the sheet   that covered Sigurd,
and placed a pillow   at Gudrun's knees:
"Look at your beloved!   Lay your lips on his,
the way you kissed   when the king was alive."

Gudrun looked   once at her lord;
she saw his hair   streaming with blood,
the keen eyes dead   in the king's face,
the great sword wound   in Sigurd's breast.

She sank to the ground   against the pillow,
her hair fell loose,   her cheeks flushed red;
drops as of rain   ran down to her knees.

Then Gjuki's daughter,   Gudrun, wept
so that the tears   streamed through her hair;
geese in the yard   began to shriek,
the famous birds   that belonged to Gudrun.

Gjuki's daughter,   Gullrond, said:
"No man and woman   in all the world
were ever given   so great a love.
Sister, I know   you never felt at peace
anywhere   away from Sigurd."

Gudrun said:
"My Sigurd was   to Gjuki's sons
as garlic stands   taller than grass,
or like a bright stone   on a string of beads,
a priceless jewel   among the princes.

"My lord's warriors   honored me once
more than any   of Odin's maids:
now I am so little,   like a winter leaf
clinging to a willow,   since the king is dead.

"I miss in the hall,   I miss in bed,
my companion   killed by Gjuki's sons,
Gjuki's sons   who gave me to grief,
who made their sister's   bitter sorrow.

"May all who live here   leave your lands
as you cast aside   the oaths you swore!
Gunnar, you'll get   no joy from the gold—
the rings will drive you   to your death,
because you swore   an oath with Sigurd.

"There was greater happiness   in this house
before my Sigurd   saddled Grani,
and they left   on a luckless day
to woo Brynhild,   the worst of women."

Then said Brynhild,   Budli's daughter:
"May she mourn   her man and children,
who taught you, Gudrun,   to shed tears,
and gave you this day   the gift of speech."

Gjuki's daughter,   Gullrond, said:
"Accursed woman,   don't speak such words!
Ever have you proved   the bane of princes,
all the world   wishes you ill;
seven kings   you've brought to sorrow,
widows you've made   of many wives."

Then said Brynhild,   Budli's daughter:
"Atli bears the guilt   of all this grief,
Atli, my brother,   Budli's son.

"Around a hero   in the Hunnish hall
flickered the light   of Fafnir's lair,
and I paid   for the prince's journey,
for that sight   I still can see."

She stood by a pillar,   summoning her strength;
fire burned   in Brynhild's eyes,
baneful venom   flew from her lips,
when she saw the wounds,   how Sigurd died.

Then Gudrun went away into the forests and through the
wilderness until she came to Denmark. There she stayed with
Thora, Hakon's daughter, for seven years. Brynhild did not want

---

all the world wishes you ill. The translation of this line is uncertain.
"Atli bears the guilt." That is, Atli coveted the gold offered as a bride-price;
but unless he was aware that Gunnar, rather than Sigurd, was to be her husband, Brynhild would have no cause for complaint.
summoning her strength. Translation uncertain.

to live on without Sigurd. She had eight of her slaves killed, and five bondmaids. Then she killed herself with her sword, as it is told in *The Short Lay of Sigurd*.

She had eight of her slaves killed. The slaves and bondmaids would accompany Brynhild to Hel and serve her there. They were necessary for her prestige—see also *The Short Lay of Sigurd,* stanzas 47–52.

THE SHORT LAY OF SIGURD

The story told mainly from Brynhild's point of view.

Sigurd the Volsung,   who had slain Fafnir,
once was a guest   in Gjuki's hall.
He swore   with Gjuki's sons,
Gunnar and Hogni,   friendship forever.

Their sister   would be Sigurd's bride,
young Gudrun,   rich in gold.
Sigurd the Volsung   and Gjuki's sons
drank and talked   many days together.

And when the brothers   went to see Brynhild,
the maiden they hoped   would marry Gunnar,
Sigurd went with them   to show the way;
he would have claimed her   himself if he could.

The warrior set   his naked sword,
blazoned with runes,   between himself and Brynhild;
the southern king   did not once kiss her
nor did he hold her   in his arms,
but gave the promised   maiden to Gunnar.

Brynhild knew   her life was blameless;
she was innocent   of any evil,
none could say   she deserved to die.
The grim Fates   wrought her grief.

Sitting outside   when the day was over,
alone, in her sorrow   she would say,
"I must have him   here in my arms,
though Sigurd die   for my desire!

Brynhild knew. . . . This stanza contains certain difficulties, but the poet's clear intention is to absolve Brynhild of any blame for the events that follow.

"Yet I am wrong   to speak such words—
Gudrun is his wife,   and I am Gunnar's;
never will the foul Norns   free us from longing."

As she sat there alone,   evil thoughts
would fill her mind   and freeze her heart
when Gudrun had gone   to bed with Sigurd,
and they were lying   under linen,
the warrior Hun   and his fair wife.

"Joyless I live,   bereft of my love;
now let hatred   soothe my heart!"

Driven by rage,   she sought revenge:
"I shall leave you, Gunnar;   before too long
you will have lost me   and all my lands;
I won't live   with a weakling lord.

"I will go back   to where I lived before,
return to my relatives,   my close kin,
stay there and sleep   my life away,
unless you demand   Sigurd's death,
and you, prince, take   the chieftain's place.

"And let his son   follow Sigurd!
A wolf-cub will not be   welcome for long:
who will sooner   seek to avenge
a father slain   than his living son?"

Gunnar was grieved   and sat in gloom,
sifting his thoughts   throughout the day,
trying to decide   what he should do—
what would best   bring him honor,
what would best   avail him now.
He had vowed friendship   with the Volsung,
and he would be sorry   to see him die.

Gunnar thought about   another thing:
never before   had a queen been known
to cast aside   her place in the kingdom.
He went to ask   his brother's advice,
sure that Hogni   could give him help.

"Of all things in life,   what I love most
is Brynhild, my bride,   the best of women;
sooner would I suffer   death itself
than lose the dowry   of Budli's daughter.

"Should we kill   our king for his treasure?
The gold of the Rhine   is good to rule—
how well we two   could wield that wealth,
sitting in peace,   enjoy that prize!"

He didn't wait long   for Hogni's words:
"We would do   ourselves dishonor
if our swords broke   the oaths we swore,
our sworn oaths   of friendship with Sigurd.

"The world does not hold   happier men
while we four prevail   to rule the people,
and the Hunnish hero   lives here among us.
No one in the world   will have worthier kin
when we five   beget fine sons,
and greater grows   the Gjuking might.

"It's easy to see why   you spoke those words:
Brynhild is raging   for revenge."

than lose the dowry. Spoken like a true Viking.

The gold of the Rhine. So called because the bottom of the river is the ultimate
destination of the Niflung hoard.

while we four prevail. The numbers in this stanza are inexplicable, as are the
"five sons" of the *Fragment of a Sigurd Lay*, stanza 8.

Gunnar said:
"Then we will use   our younger brother;
for him no dishonor   lies in the deed.
Guthorm had no share   in our sworn oaths,
the oaths we swore   to friendship with Sigurd."

Reckless Guthorm   was glad to agree;
a sword stood   in Sigurd's heart.

The hero avenged himself   there in the hall—
the reckless youth   was killed in return;
the bright sword flashed   from Sigurd's hand,
and Guthorm felt   Gram's power.

Cut in half   fell Sigurd's foe;
his arms and head   were hurled aside,
but where he had stood,   his legs sank down.

Gudrun had been   asleep in bed,
safe and content   at Sigurd's side;
but she awakened   bathed in the blood
of her dying lord,   her joy lost forever.

She struck her hands   so hard together,
the strong-minded warrior   rose and said:
"Gudrun, you must not   give way to grief;
my young bride, remember,   your brothers live.

"I have still   a son and heir
who will find it hard   to flee this hall.
My foes were led   to act like fools
when they took counsel   to have me killed.

Reckless Guthorm was glad to agree. This version omits the methods of persuasion detailed in the *Fragment of a Sigurd Lay*, stanza 4.

Remember, your brothers live. As the following stanzas show, Sigurd cannot be suggesting that Gudrun's brothers could console her, or avenge him. He must be thinking that Gudrun would have to hide her feelings.

"If their sister   bears seven sons,
none like Sigurd's   will stand beside them;
well do I know   whose need they served—
Brynhild alone   has brought them to grief.

"That maiden loved   no man but me,
and yet toward Gunnar   I have no guilt;
I did not break   the oath I swore,
not wanting to be called   the queen's lover."

Sigurd's last breath   met Gudrun's sigh;
she struck her hands   so hard together
that all the cups   clattered on the wall.
Outside in the yard   the shrill geese screamed.

And one great laugh   rang loud in the hall
when Budli's daughter,   Brynhild, could hear
as she lay in bed   the wild lament,
the woe that had come   to Sigurd's wife.

Then said Gunnar,   leader of men:
"Lusting for vengeance,   you can laugh,
but glad you are not,   nor do you find it good.
Mother of evils,   your white face
foretells your doom: you won't wait long to die.

"Woman, if we did   as you deserve,
you would see us   strike Atli down;
after he fell   before your eyes,
you would bind your brother's   bloody wounds."

Brynhild said:
"No one would deny   the deed you've done,
but Gunnar is no foe   to frighten my brother;

---

none like Sigurd's. The literal meaning of this line is: The Gjukings will have
no sons as fine as Sigurd's (would have been) to accompany them to the Thing.

his heart will be strong   when yours has stopped—
you will always   yield to his might.

"What I will tell you, Gunnar,   you know already:
yours is the guilt   for all this grief.
I was young and happy   in my brother's house,
nor was I lacking   in land or wealth.

"I did not mean   to be married ever
before you Gjukings   came as guests,
and rode into my courtyard,   three great kings—
luckless was the day   you left your lands!

"The man I thought   that I would marry
sat with the gold   on Grani's back;
his eyes   were not like yours,
he did not look   like you at all,
though you called yourselves   great kings.

"And Atli said   to me in secret
he wouldn't give up   my gold or lands
unless I married   one of those men,
nor would he part with   that great prize
of silver counted out   and kept for my dowry.

"Then my thoughts   were turned to this:
I could be a warrior   wielding death,
fighting battles   against my brother.
Thus I would do   famous deeds,
darken the minds   of many men.

"We let our talk   lead us to terms;
I would have   the dragon's hoard,
the red rings   of Sigmund's son;
I did not want the gift   of another man's gold.

"One man only   I loved, not more;
my mind was not   made to be fickle.
Atli will know   all this at last,
when he discovers   how I died—

"I will have revenge   for all my wrongs."

Up rose Gunnar,   ruler of men,
and wound his arms   around his wife;
everyone came   and spoke kind words,
urging Brynhild   to live on.

She cast aside   every caress,
let no one lead her   from the long road.

Gunnar went to Hogni,   asking for help:
"I want the men,   yours and my own,
to come to the hall—   and let them be quick!
We must find a way   to prevent the worst,
or Brynhild will die   as she now desires.
Then we can see   what time counsels."

He didn't have to wait   for Hogni's words:
"Let no one lead her   from the long road;
may her ride to Hel   have no returning!
Monstrous she came   from her mother's womb,
born to be ever   bound to evil
and bring misfortune   to many men."

Then Gunnar   turned away, grieving.
Richly adorned,   Brynhild dealt out treasure.

She looked her last   at all she owned,
the serving-women   and bondmaids slain,

"One man only. . . ." Two lines, reading "For let no woman give her love
heedlessly to another's husband," are omitted after this stanza. They are, as
Boer says, out of place.

put on gold war-gear—   glad she was not
before she thrust   the sword-blade through.

She sank down on her side   against a pillow,
wounded as she was,   to speak these words:

"I have gold   for all my handmaids
who would receive   a remembrance from me;
to each I promise   a painted necklace,
cloth richly dyed,   brightly colored dresses."

They were all silent   when she had spoken,
then all together   returned this answer:
"Enough of your servants   have been slain;
the dead bondwomen   will do you honor."

After a moment   the handmaids heard
the linen-clad woman,   so young, reply:
"I do not want   anyone unwilling
for love of me   to lose her life.

"But fewer jewels   and less fair gold
you'll have to burn   upon your bones
when you must come   to meet me in Hel.

"Gunnar, sit down!   While life yet lingers
let your fair bride   foretell your fate:
your ship will not keep   an even keel
even though Brynhild   has breathed her last.

"You'll settle with Gudrun   sooner than you think;
she will be queen   in Atli's court
and still grieve   for Sigurd's death.

"Enough of your servants. . . ." The bondwomen's answer indicates the true
meaning of Brynhild's offer.

"A maiden will be born there,   raised by her mother,
Gudrun's daughter, Swanhild;   the sun
in a cloudless sky   is not so fair.

"You will give Gudrun   to a great lord,
a warrior skilled   at wielding death.
"She will not go   to this marriage gladly;
against her wishes   she will be the wife
of Atli, my brother,   Budli's son.

"Well I remember   how I was wronged,
how you tricked me;   since that time
never again   have I known joy.

"You will want Oddrun   for your wife,
a marriage Atli   will not allow;
she will surrender   to you in secret—
I would have loved you   the way she will
if we had found   a kinder fate.

"Atli will trick you   to be avenged;
in the deep snake-pit   you will die.

"But it will happen   that Atli himself,
before too long,   will lose his life,
all his treasure,   and his two sons.
When bitter-hearted Gudrun   strikes a blow,
Atli's blood   will stain his bed.

"Gudrun, your sister,   would have sooner
followed in death   her first husband,
had she been given   good counsel,
or if she had   a heart like mine.

a warrior skilled. . . . This line is **conjectural.**
"Gudrun, your sister, would have sooner. . . ." That is, would have behaved
more worthily.

"Slowly I speak now;   but she will not
lose her life   for love of Sigurd.
On the high seas   her ship will sail
to a land where Jonacr   will be her lord.

"She will bear   Jonacr's babies;
they will inherit   all his wealth.
Then she will make   the maiden Swanhild,
Sigurd's daughter,   leave the land.

"Slandered by Bicci,   Swanhild will die
under the hooves   of Ermanarik's horses;
nothing remains   of Sigurd's race,
and Gudrun suffers   one grief more.

"Do not refuse me   this request,
Brynhild's last   desire in life:
have a broad pyre   built on a plain,
and let us all   lie there together
who go to seek   Sigurd in Hel.

"Cover the pyre   with colored hangings,
place on it shields,   and many slaves;
next to Sigurd's body   let mine burn.

"On the other side   of Sigurd burn
my serving-women   weighted with gold,
two hounds at his head,   two hawks at his feet,
so that all   is fittingly arranged.

"Set between us   the shining sword;
let the blade lie   as once before

"Slowly I speak now." "Slowly" is Finnur Jónsson's interpretation; Boer suggests "openly," "unwarily."

two hounds at his head. "hounds" supplies an obviously missing word in the text. The hounds are mentioned in the *Volsung Saga*.

when I shared   a bed with Sigurd,
and people called us   a married couple.

"Shut not yet   on Sigurd's heels
the gleaming, ring-locked   gates of Hel;
I do not follow   far behind,
nor can our company   be called unworthy.

"Five bondmaids   will follow Sigurd,
eight noble thanes   will serve him now,
with my nurse,   and all the treasure
Budli gave   his newborn child.

"I have said much,   and would say more,
if death were willing   yet to delay;
my voice grows weak,   my wounds are swelling;
you've heard the truth—   my time has come."

BRYNHILD'S JOURNEY TO HEL

Brynhild, on her way to meet Sigurd in Hel, justifies herself to a giantess.

After Brynhild's death two fires were built, and the one for Sigurd was burned first. Brynhild was burned in the other; she was in a chariot draped with costly fabric. It is said that Brynhild drove in the chariot along the road to Hel and went around a meadow where a giantess lived. The hag said:

"You shall not pass   where I have power,
where my rock fortress   rules the road!
You should sit at home   and do fine sewing,
not hurry after   another woman's husband!

"What brings you here   from the fields of battle,
fickle-hearted woman,   to find my house?
I'll tell you, fine lady,   what is true:
you've washed your gentle hands   of heroes' blood."

Then said Brynhild:
"You shall not reproach me,   bride of the rock,
though as a warrior   I once lived;
worthier than you   will I be counted
where our names   and kin are known."

The giantess said:
"You were Brynhild,   Budli's daughter,
black was the hour   when you were born—
Gjuki's sons   you brought to sorrow,
you laid waste   their lordly house."

Brynhild said:
"Now I'll tell you,   if you would know,
truth for your wild,   witless tale.

This is what I owe   to Gjuking honor:
lost love   and a broken oath.

"For vengeance the king,   Odin, kept me,
Atli's sister,   captive under shields.
If you would know,   I was twelve years old
when I swore   the oath with Sigurd.

"They called me Hild,   at home in Hlymdal;
I was a valkyrie,   vowed to war.

"I let old Hjalm-Gunnar,   lord of Goths,
be the next hero   sent to Hel;
he was beaten   by Auda's brother—
in return,   I felt Odin's wrath.

"In Scatalund   he closed shields over me,
rims touching,   red and white;
no man, he said,   should break my sleep
but one who had never   known of fear.

"Odin surrounded   my southern hall
with high flames,   fiercely burning;
the man who braved   the fire would bring
the hoard that lay   in Fafnir's lair.

"Riding Grani,   laden with gold,
he found the hall   of my foster-father;
and they deemed   that Danish viking
worthiest of all   the warriors there.

---

and a broken oath. Her own promise to marry Sigurd; the oath she was tricked into breaking. Presumably the mechanism was that described in *The Lay of Gripir:* Sigurd had the outward form of Gunnar. See also stanza 13.

"For vengeance the king. . . ." This stanza is translated in accordance with Boer's interpretation, particularly "captive under shields"; Sigurd is referred to only as "the young king" in the text.

"They called me Hild." "Hild" means "battle."

that Danish viking. "Danish" is simply honorific.

"We lay together   in one bed
as if we two   were brother and sister;
not though we slept   for eight nights so
did one of us ever   touch the other.

"But one day Gudrun,   Gjuki's daughter,
claimed I had slept   in Sigurd's arms.
What I learned then   I did not want to know:
they had tricked me   when I married.

"For men and women   born in the world
life is bitter   and lasts too long.
But never will we   be parted now,
Sigurd and I, hag—   be gone from my sight!'

be gone from my sight! "Be gone" translates "sink down," as at the end of
The Sibyl's Prophecy.

THE SECOND LAY OF GUDRUN

Gudrun relates Sigurd's death, her marriage to Atli and her life with him. The greater age of this poem, called The Old Lay of Gudrun, *probably accounts for the gaps and confusion in the text.*

My mother brought me up,   a peerless maiden;
my life was happy,   I loved my brothers,
until the day Gjuki   dowered me with gold,
dowered me with gold   and gave me to Sigurd.

But my brothers   could not bear
to see my husband   foremost of men;
they could not sleep   or sit in council
until their swords   had slain Sigurd.

Grani galloped home—   I heard his hoofs,
but Sigurd himself   I could not see;
the saddle horses   were dark with sweat,
hard work they had,   carrying the killers.

In tears, I went   to talk to Grani,
weeping, I asked him   what had happened;
sadly then Grani   let his head sink to the ground,
the horse knew   his master was no more.

Long I waited,   long I wondered
before I questioned   the king about Sigurd.

The Second Lay of Gudrun. A prose passage preceding the first stanza tells us that Gudrun is speaking to Thjodrek in Atli's court.

and gave me to Sigurd. Stanza 2 is omitted; it is essentially repeated in *The First Lay of Gudrun,* and although the *Second Lay* is presumably older, the comparison of Sigurd to a garlic in the grass, a tall stag among deer, and red gold against grey silver interrupts here and occurs appropriately there.

Grani galloped home. The correct reading may be that Grani was galloping *to,* rather than *from,* the Thing. In either case, the murder in this version did not occur in the hall.

the saddle horses. Gudrun's brothers' horses, when they returned.

Gunnar bowed his head,   but Hogni told me
how the warrior   died of wounds:
"He lies struck down   beyond the Rhine;
wolves claim the body   of Guthorm's bane.

"Go look for Sigurd   in the South!
You'll hear the sound of ravens screaming,
eagles screaming,   eager to feed,
wolves howling   around your husband."

"How can you tell me   such tidings,
Hogni, speak words   so terrible to hear?
I hope that the ravens   tear your heart out
where you wander   wide lands alone."

Hogni answered   only this,
not rejoicing,   with great sorrow:
"Gudrun, it would only   grieve you more
if hungry ravens   fed on my heart."

Hearing that answer,   I turned away
to search the woods   for what the wolves had left.

There was no moon   in the black night
as I sat in sorrow   over Sigurd;
I wished,   hearing the wolves,
that they would come   and kill me too.

I followed the mountains   five full days;
then I came   to Half's high hall.

beyond the Rhine. Literally, "beyond the sea."
Guthorm's bane. Guthorm is elsewhere, and probably here too, Sigurd's killer.
where you wander. . . . This line is conjectural.
. . . for what the wolves had left. Three lines are omitted after this one, as Boer
recommends. They occur in the first stanza of *The First Lay of Gudrun.*
. . . and kill me too. The line following this is very unclear, and has been
omitted.

I stayed with Thora   for seven seasons,
lived in Denmark   with Hakon's daughter;
to gladden me,   she embroidered in gold
Danish swans   and southern halls.

We portrayed   the play of men,
the king's warriors,   finely worked,
red shields,   and the ranks of Huns,
sword-bearing, helmeted   hosts of the king.

[handwritten margin notes: Hakon Jarl - supporter of paganism. Thora - there Hakon's daughter - in other sources his wife]

Sigmund's ships   were gliding from the shore,
their gleaming prows   inlaid with gold,
and we embroidered   the great battle
of Sigar and Siggeir   south in Fjon.

The Gothic queen,   Grimhild, learned
where I was . . . .
put down her sewing   and called her sons;
urgently   she asked them this:
would they make amends   for their sister's son,
compensate Gudrun   for killing her husband?

Gunnar said   he would give me gold
to settle the claim;   and so said Hogni.
Then Grimhild asked   who would go
saddle the horses   and hitch the wagon.

for seven seasons. Seven years, or, more probably here, seven half-years.
and southern halls. That is, Danish halls.
the play of men: warfare.
where I was. . . . We have only half of the line, and the meaning of that is uncertain.
would they make amends. The danger Sigurd anticipates in the *Short Lay,* stanza 26, would seem to have been realized.
Then Grimhild asked. Grimhild is probably asking if they will accompany her to Denmark. It is not really clear whether they do or not. Two lines, obviously out of place, follow this stanza.
and hitch the wagon. After this, stanza 19 has been omitted, as Boer suggests. It is either out of place or requires a missing stanza to explain it.

Each of them came   with costly things,
costly things   and words of kindness,
trying to console me   for my sorrow
and win a truce,   but I didn't trust them.

Then Grimhild handed me   a full horn to drink,
cool and bitter,   that cast out grief;
in it was mixed   the might of Earth,
the ice-cold sea,   and the blood of swine.

Carved on the horn   were many runes
painted red—   I could not read them—
a long serpent   out of the sea,
an ear of corn,   entrails of beasts.

Baleful things   were mixed in that beer,
herbs from the forest,   fire-blackened acorns,
the hearth's dew, soot,   entrails of sacrifices,
boiled swine's liver,   soothing to sorrow.

Then I forgot   that I had seen
the hero, Sigurd,   slain in the hall;
three kings came   to kneel before me,
afterwards Grimhild   spoke again:

"Gudrun, I will give you   much gold,
your dead father's   finest treasures,
red rings,   and Hlothver's halls,
the wall hangings   that belonged to the warrior.

---

an ear of corn. By Bugge's ingenious interpretation, the ear of corn becomes seaweed. It is, in any case, an "unreaped" ear.

Then I forgot. . . . The second part of this line is conjectural.

slain in the hall. If this is the correct interpretation of this line, it contradicts the implication of Stanza 4 as to where the killing took place.

three kings: suitors.

the wall hangings. This line is conjectural.

"You'll have Hunnish bondmaids   to weave fair linen,
embroider in gold   for your delight,
all Budli's wealth   shall belong to you,
dowered with gold   you'll be given to Atli."

"I don't want to have   another husband,
nor to be the wife   of Brynhild's brother;
I must not marry   Budli's son,
bear him children,   live a happy life."

"Don't keep on hating,   hoping for revenge,
although it is true   we wronged you once.
You'll be happy again   as if they were alive,
Sigurd and Sigmund,   if you have sons."

"Grimhild, I cannot   look glad,
nor can I hold out   hope to that hero,
since Sigurd died   and ravens sat
beside the wolves   to drink from his wounds."

"Atli is   the noblest of all
princes in the world,   the foremost warrior;
if you refuse him,   the rest of your days
you'll have to live   without a husband."

"Stop offering me   the worst of evils,
don't speak in favor   of that foul race!
Atli will do   great harm to Gunnar,
and have Hogni's   heart cut out.
I won't rest   before that reckless
lover of battle   loses his life."

Weeping, Grimhild   heard the grief to come:
her sons would find   an evil fate,
her boys would meet   only misfortune.

Sigurd and Sigmund. "Sigmund" here may refer to Sigurd's son rather than to his father.

"I'll give you more lands   and those who live there,
Vinbjorg, Valbjorg,   if you will take them,
your own to enjoy   always, my daughter!"

"Then I will agree   to marry Atli—
follow your wish   against my will; —   *important in Atli days in regards to Gudrun's revenge*
I will not find him   a husband to love,
nor will my brothers' bane   shelter my sons."

Quickly the Huns   mounted their horses,
wagons were ready   for their wives;
for seven long days   we rode the cold land,   } *in other sources journey is very long.*
seven more   we spent on the sea.
The last week we crossed   a waterless country.)

Then guards   opened the gates
of Atli's fortress   to let us in.

Atli awakened me,   but I remembered
my murdered brothers,   and hatred filled my mind.

"Just now   the Norns woke me."
He asked me to explain   prophecies of evil.
"I dreamed that you, Gudrun,   Gjuki's daughter,
pierced me through   with a poisoned sword."

"To dream of iron   foretells a fire,
a woman's fury   means willful pride.
I will burn you   to treat some illness,
comfort and cure you,   though I care not for your pain."

"I'll give you more lands." One would have expected Grimhild, who seems to
have believed Gudrun's prophecies, to act differently. It also seems unlikely that
Gudrun would have been persuaded by bribes alone.
Then guards opened. . . . Part of this stanza is missing.
Atli awakened me. From here on, the stanzas may be part of another poem.

"I thought two young trees   fell in the yard
where I would gladly   have let them grow;
torn up by the roots,   red with blood,
they were brought to the bench,   and you bade me eat them."

"I thought that from my hand   two hawks flew,
hungry for prey,   to the house of woe;
I thought I ate their hearts   sweetened with honey,
grieved in my mind,   gorged with blood.

"I dreamed that my hand   freed two young dogs,
wretchedly unhappy,   howling in fear;
I thought their flesh   became foul carrion,
and I ate the food   that is forbidden."

"The men will soon   row out to sea
and slice the heads off   shining fish;
before daybreak   enough will die,
in a few night's time,   to feed many people."

Afterwards I stayed there   not sleeping,
and refused to get up—   that I well remember.

"The men will soon. . . ." The translation follows Boer's interpretation of this
stanza.

Afterwards I stayed there. Some editors consider the last stanza to be spoken
by Atli.

THE THIRD LAY OF GUDRUN

Gudrun, suspected of infidelity to Atli, proves her innocence by ordeal.

Atli had a bondmaid named Herkja who had been his mistress. She told Atli that she had seen Thjodrek and Gudrun together. From that time on, Atli was cheerless. Then Gudrun said:

"What is wrong, Atli?   Why are you always
low in spirits,   never laughing?
Your noble warriors   wonder why
you are silent   and seem to shun me."

Atli said:
"I am grieved, Gudrun,   Gjuki's daughter,
by what Herkja told me   in the hall:
that you slept with Thjodrek,   Thjodmar's son,
lay with the warrior   gladly for love."

Gudrun said:
"I will give you   my solemn oath,
swear on the white   holy stones,
that never did I sleep   with Thjodmar's son,
we two have done   no shameful deed.

"I put my arms   around his neck
one time,   and never again;
the two of us   met only to talk
and share in secret   bitter sorrows.

"Thjodrek came here   with thirty men.
Not one of thirty   remains alive.

I put my arms. . . . Boer quotes *Thjodrek's Saga* in support of these lines, which would then refer to Gudrun's warmly greeting Thjodrek when he first arrived at Atli's court.

share in secret bitter sorrows. Presumably the stanza that follows gives the subject of their sad conversations.

You've robbed me of kinsmen   and mail-clad warriors,
you've robbed me of all   my close relations.

"Send to Saxi   the southern king!
He can bless   the boiling cauldron."
Seven hundred men   went into the hall
before the queen   put her hand in the kettle.

Gudrun said:
"Gunnar will not come now,   I can't call Hogni,
my sweet brothers   I'll never see again;
Hogni's sword   would avenge my shame—
now I must prove   my innocence myself."

She put her white hand   into the water
and gathered up   the glittering gems:
"My lords, you have seen   the sacred trial
prove me guiltless—   and still the water boils."

Atli's heart   laughed in his breast
because Gudrun's hands   had not been harmed:
"Now let Herkja   go to the kettle,
she who hoped   to hurt my wife."

No man has seen   a pitiful sight
who has not looked at   Herkja's scalded hands;
then they forced her   into a foul swamp—
Gudrun's grievance   was well avenged.

ODDRUN'S LAMENT

Atli's sister Oddrun tells of her love for Gunnar, yet another motive for Atli's hatred of the Gjukings.

King Heidrek's daughter Borgny had a lover called Vilmund. She could not give birth to her child until Oddrun, Atli's sister, came to help her. Oddrun had been the mistress of Gunnar, Gjuki's son.

In old tales   I have heard it told
that a maiden came   to Mornaland
when no one else   in all the world
could be any help   to Heidrek's daughter.

When Atli's sister   Oddrun learned
that Borgny had lain   so long in labor,
she put a bridle   on a black horse,
led it from the stall,   put on its saddle.

Then she raced   along the smooth roads
until she came   to King Heidrek's hall;
she swept the saddle   from her slender horse,
walked right in   the length of the room
and, wasting not a moment,   spoke these words:

"What is the news   of Heidrek's court?
What is happening   here in Hunland?"

A bondmaid said:
"Borgny suffers   hard birth pains, Oddrun—
can't you find a way   to help your friend?"

Oddrun said:
"Who is to blame   for Borgny's sorrow,
Why does she labor   so long in pain?"

The bondmaid said:
"Vilmund is the name   of the valiant lord

who lay with Borgny   in a warm bed
for five years,   and her father never knew."

Then they talked   no more together;
Oddrun went to Borgny   and brought her help,
chanting strong spells   and magic charms,
mighty witchcraft   for the woman's need.

A boy and a girl   were born into the world,
sweet babies   of Hogni's bane;
then the sick woman   began to speak—
not one word   had she uttered before:

"May the holy gods   help you, Oddrun,
Frigg and Freyja   and all the others,
just as you delivered me   from death this day."

Oddrun said:
"I did not come here   wanting to help you—
when was your life   worth the saving?
But what I promise,   I perform:
I pledged my skills   to all who suffer."

Borgny said:
"You're insane, Oddrun,   out of your senses,
to speak so wildly   words of hate;
I have always felt   as fond of you
as if we were born   of two brothers."

Oddrun said:
"I remember still   what you said one evening
when I gave   a drink to Gunnar:
that no one had ever   in all the world
set a worse example   for other women."

Hogni's bane. The idea that Vilmund killed Hogni is peculiar to this poem.
"I did not come here." An apparently meaningless line, reading "When the princes divided treasures," has been omitted from this stanza.

Then she sat down,   so heavy-hearted
she had to speak   about her sorrows.

"I grew up   among great lords—
most were kind to me—   in a king's hall.
For five years   while my father lived,
I rejoiced   in life and riches.

"With his last breath   that weary lord
spoke his heart's desire   before he died:
I was dowered   with red gold,
given in marriage   to Grimhild's son.

"And the king   commanded that Brynhild
wear a helmet,   become a warrior;
he said no better   maiden would be born
in all the world   as long as she lived.

"Brynhild sat weaving   among the women;
she was the lord   of lands and men.
Lightning struck   the earth and sky
when Fafnir's bane   looked at her fortress.

"When Sigurd's sword   won the victory,
Brynhild's fortress   was forced to surrender;
it was only   a short time after
that she found out   about the fraud.

"She resolved   to have revenge,
as we all discovered   to our woe;
people will learn   in every land
how Brynhild destroyed herself   when Sigurd died.

while my father lived. That is, Budli.
Grimhild's son: Gunnar.
Lightning struck. . . . Literally, "The earth and heavens shook when Fafnir's bane (Sigurd). . . ."
about the fraud. That by which she was persuaded to marry Gunnar.

"I gave   my love to Gunnar,
the noble prince,   in Brynhild's place.

"The Gjukings offered   my brother Atli
precious rings   to pay for Brynhild;
Gunnar would give   fifteen farms
and the Niflung hoard   to be my husband.

"Atli said   he would not accept
any settlement   with Gjuki's sons;
but we were not strong enough   to strive with love,
I could not deny   Gunnar's desire.

"Many of my kinsmen   came to Atli
trying to tell him   about us two;
but my brother   believed we were blameless,
that I would never do   a shameful deed.

"No one should speak   with certainty
of what is possible   for people in love.

"At last Atli   sent his spies
through the dark forest   to find the truth;
they saw us   in our secret place,
both of us lying   in one bed.

"The thanes received   red rings,
bribes to keep them   from telling my brother;
but they rushed home   in angry haste,
eager to tell   their news to Atli.

"They took care   to keep it from Gudrun,
who might have helped us   had she known.

"Golden hooves echoed   in the courtyard
when Gjuki's sons   came to visit Atli.

He had Hogni's   heart cut out;
Gunnar soon lay   among the snakes.

"I had gone   to Geirmund's house,
as often before,   to brew his beer.
Among the serpents   Gunnar struck his harp
because he hoped   that I would help him;
the noble king   thought I would come.

"I was at Hlessey,   and I heard
with what sorrow   those strings resounded.
I told my maids   to make ready at once—
I longed to save   the prince's life.

"We sailed quickly   across the Sound;
then we arrived   at Atli's hall.

"But so swiftly   slithered out
Atli's wretched mother—   may she rot!—
and sank her teeth   into Gunnar's heart
that I had no hope   of saving the hero.

"I have often wondered,   gold-decked woman,
how I can still   cling to life
when I loved   that noble lord,
that matchless hero,   as myself.

"You have sat here   and heard me talk
about misfortune,   mine and theirs;
we all live   as our loves would have us—
this is the end   of Oddrun's lament."

Atli's wretched mother. She slithered because she was in the form of a snake.

Gunnar and Hogni are killed in Atli's court, and Gudrun avenges them.

Atli sent   a trusted messenger,
Knefrodr by name,   to ride to Gunnar.
He came to Gjuki's court;   in Gunnar's hall
where benches ringed the hearth   he drank sweet beer.

The Gjukings, wary,   watching the Hun,
drank in silence   and kept their thoughts secret.
From the high seat   the southern warrior,
Knefrodr, called out   in a cold voice:

"From Atli comes   the message I carried,
spurring my swift horse,   through Mirkwood the Unknown:
let Gunnar and Hogni   put on their gilded helmets,
and leave this hearth   for Atli's home.

"There shall you choose   shields and ash-spears,
gold-trimmed helmets,   Hunnish warriors,
silver saddles,   blood-red shirts,
spears and darts,   high-spirited horses.

"The wide valley, Gnitaheath,   he'll give you,
ringing spears   and gilded ships,
a hoard of treasure,   the halls of Danp,
the great forest   men call Mirkwood."

Gunnar turned his head   and spoke to Hogni:
"What do you say,   my youngest brother?

The Lay of Atli. The word "Greenland" has been omitted from the title of this poem, to avoid confusion with the *Atlamal,* here called *The Greenland Lay of Atli,* which really was written in that country. This poem is the older of the two.
their gilded helmets. Literally "ringed," probably meaning decorated with rings.
and gilded ships. "Ships" is simply "prows" in the text.
the halls of Danp. Meaning uncertain.

I know of no gold   in Gnitaheath
so fine that we   should forget our own.

"We have seven halls   stacked with swords,
on each sword gleams   a hilt of gold;
my horse is the swiftest,   my sword the sharpest,
my bow the most supple,   my chain-mail is gold,
steel shields and helmets   that came from Kjar's halls—
any one I have   beats all of the Huns'."

Hogni said:
"What did it mean   when our sister sent us
a ring wrapped in wolf-skin?   She bids us beware.
Hairs of the heath-runner   wound on the ring
tell me that wolves   wait along our way."

*heath-runner-
wolf
(kenning)*

No one was urging   Gunnar to go,
not kinsmen, or lords,   or readers of runes;
then spoke Gunnar   as a king should,
proud, in his mead-hall,   a mighty warrior:

"Fjornir, arise!   Fill the golden horns
with good wine   for every warrior!

To grey-coated wolves,   if Gunnar dies,
let the Niflungs   leave their gold!
May black bears   turn and bite
the hound packs of men,   if Gunnar won't be home!"

The proud people, weeping,   led the prince,
ready now for battle,   out of the Niflung hall;
spoke then the youngest   of Hogni's sons:
"Fare well and safely   wherever you go!"

my bow the most supple. "Supple" translates "bench-worthy."
from Kjar's halls. Kjar is unknown.
To grey-coated wolves. The spirit of the stanza is obvious but its meaning is
rather obscure.

Then the hooves   of high-spirited horses
hammered the heath   of Mirkwood the Unknown;
all Hunland trembled   as hard-minded warriors
swept at a gallop   over fair green fields.

They saw Atli's land   and lofty halls,
followers of Budli   defending the fortress;
inside, on the wall,   between the seat-beams,
were white shields   rimmed with metal,
darts and spears.   Atli sat drinking
there in his great hall;   guards were at the door
waiting lest Gunnar's   warriors should come
with ringing spears,   ready to fight.

Gudrun, their sister,   was the first to see
her two brothers;   she had drunk little beer:
"Gunnar, you are lost.   What good will be your might
against the Hunnish evil?   Turn back at once!

"Better had you come,   brother, in war-gear,
helmed and in armor,   to seek Atli's home,
to sit in the saddle   through sun-bright days
while Norns weep   for the wan Huns dead,
their shield-maids stricken   with harrowing sorrow.
You might have put Atli   into the snake-pit,
the snake-pit he has   prepared for you."

"Too late, sister,   to summon the Niflungs,
too long to wait   for our fearless warriors
to ride through the hills   beyond the Rhine."

They fell on Gunnar   and fettered his feet;
the lord of the Burgundians   they bound fast.

Hogni slew seven   with his swift sword,
and flung the eighth   into the blazing fire;

so shall a warrior   drive back his foes,
as Hogni fought,   defending Gunnar.

They asked Gunnar,   lord of the Goths,
if he would buy   his life with gold.

"Let Hogni's heart   lie in my hands,
bloody as it came   from the hero's breast;
let a sharp sword   cleave Gjuki's son."

They cut the heart   from Hjalli's breast,
and brought it, bloody,   in a bowl to Gunnar.

Then said Gunnar,   ruler of men:
"This is the heart   of craven Hjalli,
not like the heart   of Hogni the brave;
it trembles badly,   lying in the bowl,
but half as much   as where it lay before."

Hogni laughed   when they cut out his heart—
He could not be   a quaking coward.
They brought his heart, bloody,   in a bowl to Gunnar.

Then said Gunnar,   spear of the Niflungs:
"This is the heart   of Hogni the brave,
not like the heart   of craven Hjalli:
little does it tremble,   lying in the bowl,
but it trembled less   where it lay before.

"You shall lose   your life, Atli,
just as you've lost   all hope of the treasure!
In my hands alone   is the hidden gold,
the hoard of the Niflungs: Hogni is dead."

While two of us shared it,   I could not be sure,
but what I choose now   nothing can change:

"You shall lose your life." This translates a phrase of uncertain meaning.

The Rhine shall rule   the ore of strife,
the rapid river   shall be the Niflung heir;
under rolling waters   shine the deadly rings,
hidden forever   from the hands of Huns."

Atli said:
"Drive on the carts!   The captive is in chains."

The mighty Atli   mounted Glaum
and rode away,   his warriors around him.
Gudrun invoked   the gods of war;
holding back tears,   she came into the hall.

"May you be granted, Atli,   what you to Gunnar
swore in many oaths   and often vowed
by the sun in the southlands,   by Sigtyr's rock—
the god's resting place—   and by Ull's ring."

But at that moment,   the master of the gold
was being dragged   toward his death.

Alive into   the slithering pit
a crowd of men   lowered the king;
but Gunnar, alone   among the serpents
struck his harp   with wrathful hands.
The strings resounded.   So shall a war-lord
defend his treasure   against his foes.

Atli spurred   his swift horse
and galloped home   after Gunnar's murder;
hoofs clattered   in the crowded yard,
weapons clashed, as Huns   returned from the heath.

Gudrun came   to welcome Atli,
offered the king   a gilded cup:

"Drive on the carts! . . ." Stanzas 28 through 31 are arranged as in Boer.
Gudrun invoked. . . . "Invoked" replaces a missing half-line.

"My lord, in your hall   let Gudrun's hands
make you merry   with fresh young meat!"

Ale-cups echoed,   heavy with wine,
as Huns assembled   in Atli's hall;
long-bearded warriors   made haste to come.

Bright-faced Gudrun   served them drink;
to the yellow-beaked warrior,   against her will,
she offered ale-dainties,   then reviled Atli:

"Now has the sword-wielder   eaten his sons'
gory hearts   made sweet with honey!
Digest the ale-dainties   of dead men's flesh
sent to your high-seat,   that, drunk, you devoured!

Never again   will you call to your knees
Erp and Eitil,   merry with ale;
never will you see   the princes at their sports,
dividing war-spoils,   fitting shafts to spears,
trimming manes,   spurring their swift horses."

A strange murmur   came from the men;
warriors cried out   and wept aloud.
Only Gudrun   gave no tears
to her bear-hearted brothers   or the sweet boys,
the innocent sons   she bore to Atli.

make you merry. This line attempts to render the intention of this obscure passage, in which Gudrun seems as sinister to the reader as she seems courteous to her husband.

the yellow-beaked warrior. The Huns were often said to be yellow-skinned; earlier, in stanza 16, they are spoken of as "pale." I follow Boer's reading of this line as referring to Atli alone, he being thus the only one to whom Gudrun offered the children's flesh.

sent to your high-seat. In ancient halls the benches were placed along each of the long walls, with a place of honor, "high seat" with ornamental sides, in the middle of each, one for the host and one for the most honored guest.

Erp and Eitil. Atli's sons. It does seem to be they who were merry, not Atli.

The swan-white lady   scattered gold,
with red rings   she enriched the warriors,
hastened their fate   as she flung bright metal—
she did not spare   the treasure-stores.

Atli, unwary,   had drunk himself weak;
he had no weapon   to ward off Gudrun—
many times the princes   had seen these two
softly embracing   in that same hall.

Gudrun held a spike   in murderous hands;
the bed drank blood.   She let loose the dogs,
and ran to wake up   the warriors in the hall
with a burning brand: they paid for her brothers.

She gave to the flames   all those she found inside
who from the murders   had come out of Mirkwood;
old timbers fell,   treasure houses filled with smoke,
the Budling fortress   burned, and inside
the doomed shield-maids   died in the flames.

The tale has been told.   Never since that time
has a woman wrought   such revenge for her brothers;
three great kings   Gudrun the fair
sent to their deaths   before she died.

THE GREENLAND LAY OF ATLI

A more deliberately literary version of the Atli story by a poet from Greenland. The translation attempts to reproduce the peculiar rhythm of the poem, in which nearly all the lines, including the half-lines, end on an unaccented syllable.

It's a well-known story   how Atli's warriors,
feasting together,   started trouble.
What they said in secret   they suffered for later;
so did the sons of Gjuki,   betrayed and slaughtered.

Their evil plotting   doomed the princes;
Atli had considered,   but gave bad counsel—
to slay his own supporters   would make him weaker—
he called his wife's brothers,   said they must come quickly.

Clever Gudrun   contrived to help them—
she overheard   what Atli intended,
but couldn't find a way   to send a warning:
his ship would sail,   and she'd be left behind.

She carved a message,   and Vingi concealed it—
this he did for Gudrun—   before he departed;
then Atli's messengers   sailed away
across the water   to find the warriors.

The Gjukings welcomed them;   fires were kindled,
no one mistrusted   the messengers from Atli;
they took the gifts,   weapons from Gudrun,
hung them up quickly,   and did not heed their warning.

Hogni's wife, Kostbera,   welcomed the messengers,
a cheerful woman,   she greeted them warmly;

Vingi concealed it. That is, contorted it; or it may be that Vingi merely gave the confused message to those who were to sail.

weapons from Gudrun. The warning must have been scratched onto one of the weapons.

Gunnar's wife, Glaumvor,   was glad to see them,
and gave them everything   guests would need.

Hogni was to sail with them—   they hoped to lure Gunnar—
he would have understood it,   had his eyes been open.
Gunnar promised   to go if Hogni wished to;
Hogni would do   as his brother decided.

The women brought them mead,   the meat was plentiful,
full horns went around   until all were contented.
Everyone retired   when he was ready.

Kostbera was learned,   she could read runes;
she spelled out the letters   there in the firelight,
kept her tongue guarded,   trying to understand them;
so blurred was the message   she couldn't tell its meaning.

She and Hogni   went to bed later.
Kostbera had a dream;   she did not conceal it
but said to her husband   as soon as she awakened:

"You plan to travel, Hogni;   take my advice—
few can give good counsel—   go another time!
I have read the runes   written by your sister:
the fair Gudrun   won't welcome guests of Atli.

"One thing troubles me—   I can't understand it—
for what reason   were the runes miswritten?
Beneath the message   was a hidden meaning:
if you two came to Atli,   you would both be killed.
Gudrun's runes are faulty,   or another wrote them."

Hogni said:
"Women always worry—   this is not wisdom;
I'll look for trouble   when it's time to take revenge;

few can give good counsel. That is, few can read runes.

the king will give us gold   red as glowing embers—
fearful omens   have never frightened me."

Kostbera said:
"You'll reach Atli's hall   only to regret it,
this time you'll find there   no friendly welcome.
Hogni, what I dreamed   I will not hide from you:
your journey is ill-fated,   and I'm afraid.

"I saw your bed-clothes   all on fire, blazing;
high flames were leaping   against my house."

Hogni said:
"Linen things that lie here   and seem of small importance
may blaze up suddenly   just like the bed-clothes."

Kostbera said:
"I thought a bear came in here;   the walls were broken;
his paws threatened us   and we were afraid,
his mouth caught many   and we could not fight him,
the hall trembled   with terrible trampling."

Hogni said:
"The wind will grow stronger,   the weather will be frightening;
the white bear you saw   means a storm from the east."

Kostbera said:
"I saw an eagle flying   straight through the hall—
surely a bad omen—   he sprinkled us with blood.
He seemed to rage at us;   I thought it was Atli."

Hogni said:
"Soon we'll be slaughtering—   then we'll see redness;
we often dream of eagles   meaning oxen;
Atli desires no evil,   whatever you may dream."

"I saw an eagle flying." Kostbera thought it was Atli's *hamr*—his "form" or spirit—a kind of ghost of the living.

Thus their talk ended;   they spoke no more about it.

The others awakened   and spoke in the same way:
Glaumvor told her husband   dreams that were hateful,
and Gunnar attempted   to give them a good meaning.

Glaumvor said:
"I saw you going   to be hung on a gallows,
snakes ate you alive,   they slithered over you,
the world came to an end;   what can be the meaning?"

Glaumvor said:
"I saw a bloody sword   drawn from your shirt—
such dreams are terrible   to tell a husband—
a spear had been thrust   through your body,
and at both ends of it   wolves were howling."

Gunnar said:
"Little dogs run about   barking loudly;
hounds will make merry   before a battle."

Glaumvor said:
"I saw a river   running through the hall.
It roared in anger,   rushed between the benches,
and both you brothers   had your legs broken;
nothing stopped the waters—   that must mean something."

Glaumvor said:
"I saw dead women   here in the darkness;
dressed in fine clothing;   they came to summon you,
bade you hasten   to their halls.
I think the guardian spirits   have gone from you forever."

---

and Gunnar attempted. The lacuna in the last line has been filled according
to Boer.
"what can be the meaning?" Stanzas 23 and 27, which would give Gunnar's re-
plies, are missing.

Gunnar said:
"There's nothing to discuss— it's all decided.
We said we would go and I won't turn away,
although it seems likely we won't live much longer."

Early in the morning the men got up,
eager to be off; others tried to warn them.
There were five travelers with only twice as many
of their household warriors; that was not wisdom.

There were Snaevar and Solar, the sons of Hogni,
and then they called on Orkning to come with them too—
glad was the warrior— Hogni's wife's brother.

The women went with them as far as the water,
the lovely ones still warning, the warriors not listening.

Gunnar's wife Glaumvor talked to Vingi,
speaking the words that she wanted to say:
"I don't know how you're planning to repay our welcome,
but hateful is the guest who harms his host."

Vingi swore to her— he did not spare himself—
"May giants take anyone who tells you lies.
May whoever breaks this peace hang on the gallows!"

Then said Bera, glad to believe him:
"May you sail safely and be successful,
go, with my good wishes, may all be well."

Hogni answered— he loved his family—
"Hope for the best, whatever may befall us,
though men have come to grief despite good wishes:
a traveler's leavetaking may help him little."

They looked at each other for the last time;
their destinies from then on were divided.

They rowed so mightily   they almost ripped the keel off,
bending over backwards,   reaching out in rage;
they split the oar-straps,   smashed the pins,
left the ship unfastened   when they landed.

A little later—   I'll shorten a long story—
they saw buildings   which belonged to Budli;
the gate creaked noisily   under Hogni's knocking.

Then Vingi said   what he should have kept silent:
"Leave this house quickly!   Danger is hidden here!
Soon I'll see you burning,   soon you'll be struck down!
Fair words brought you here—   they had a foul meaning;
keep on this road   and I'll have your gallows ready."

These words said Hogni—   he never would give way,
nor was he fearful   of what was fated:
"Don't try to scare us,   you won't succeed!
Say another word   and you'll be sorry."

They struck down Vingi   and sent him to Hel,
butchered him with axes   while his last breath rattled.

Atli's men marched forward   dressed in armor;
and faced Hogni's warriors;   a wall stood between them.
They shouted angrily,   all together:
"We've been expecting you,   you won't escape alive!"

Hogni said:
"If you've been expecting us,   you should be ashamed
to let a blow from our side   begin the battle—

they split the oar-straps. The significance of these destructive gestures must
lie in the Norse preference for making sure the battle is lost in advance.
They struck down Vingi. Either the poet or Hogni must have become impatient.

one of your warriors   is on his way to Hel!''
Their foes' mockery   made them furious;
fingers stretched out   to grasp at bowstrings.
They shot sharply   and ducked behind their shields.

Those in the house   heard what was happening;
outside the door a servant   shouted aloud.

Then was Gudrun   dreadful in her grieving,
she flung her necklace   so hard to the floor
that the rings of silver   split and broke apart.

She opened wide the doors,   and went outside;
she was calm   as she welcomed her kinsmen,
turned to greet her brothers   for the last time,
and spoke these words   to the Niflungs as well:

''I tried to help you,   urged you to stay home,
but fate can't be conquered;   you had to come here.''
She spoke wisely,   wanting them reconciled,
but they would not be counseled,   kept on saying no.

Seeing there was no way   to stop the bloodshed,
calling on all her courage,   she cast aside her cloak,
unsheathed a sword,   and struck for her kinsmen,
laid her hand   where the fight was hottest.
Gjuki's daughter   felled two bold warriors:
Atli's brother   was carried from the battlefield;
she struck so fiercely   she cut his foot from under him.

When she struck another,   he didn't stand again;
to Hel she sent him,   and her hands did not tremble.

Their valiant fighting   made them famous,
outdid all the other   deeds of the Gjukings;
it was said that the Niflungs,   as long as they survived,

struck great sword blows,   slit through byrnies,
hewed at helmets: their strength was in their hearts.

They fought all morning   until past midday,
all night long   and into the next day;
before they were finished   the field ran with blood,
the three had defeated   eighteen before they fell,
Bera's two sons   and her valiant brother.

Thus Atli   spoke in his anger:
"This is an evil sight,   and all your doing;
we were thirty warriors,   thanes full of valor.
Only eleven   are still alive.

"We were four brothers   when we lost Budli;
half are in Hel now—   two lie here struck down.

"A mighty family   is mine by marriage
with a hateful woman   who never made me happy.
Peace I've known but seldom   since I possessed you,
you've killed my kinsmen,   cost me much treasure,
sent to Hel my sister—   that's my worst sorrow."

Gudrun said:
"You dare to accuse me!   Have you forgotten, Atli?
You took my mother   and murdered her for treasure,
my wise cousin   you starved inside a cave.
My heart rejoices   when you relate your sorrows.
I give thanks to the gods   when your life goes badly."

Atli said:
"My lords, I ask you   to add to the grievances
of this great woman—   make my wife suffer!
I want to witness   Gudrun's weeping;
I want to see her   weighed down with sorrow.

"We were four brothers . . ." Boer gives five, not four.
You took my mother. Gudrun's accusations in this stanza are unsupported.

"Seize Hogni,   stick a knife into him,
carve his breast out   as I command you!
String up fierce Gunnar   on a high gallows;
dare this brave deed: drop him in the snake pit!"

Hogni said:
"Do as it pleases you,   I'll endure it gladly,
I'll show you courage—   I've suffered worse before.
We hurt you badly   when we were whole;
now that we're wounded,   even you can win."

Beiti spoke—   he was Atli's bailiff:
"Let's kill Hjalli   instead of Hogni,
do our work half way—   he's fit for dying;
that lousy weakling   need live no longer!"

The cook was terrified,   he ran out of the room;
that born coward   crammed himself into corners,
and cursed the quarrel   that caused him such misery,
ending his dreary days   dragged from his pigsty
to lose the good things   that life had offered.

They captured Hjalli   and held a knife over him;
the thrall began pleading   before he felt the point,
yelled that he'd find time enough   to dung the yard,
he'd do the filthiest work   if he were free again,
he'd be joyful   just to keep on living.

Hogni protested—   few people would have done so—
spoke up for Hjalli,   wanting him set free:
"It would be better   to finish our business—
why should we stay here   and listen to him shriek?"

They seized the warrior—   there was no other way—
they couldn't let the hero   live any longer;

dragged from his pigsty. Hjalli had tended the pigs.

laughed then Hogni— all the men heard him—
he knew how to steel himself   to stand the torture.

Gunnar took his harp,   and using his toes
played so skillfully   the women sobbed,
and all the warriors   wept if they heard him
tell Gudrun he was dying;   the rafters gave way.

The two brave men died   early in the morning;
as long as their hearts beat   they were heroes.

Full of pride was Atli,   he'd overcome them both;
he told her grief to Gudrun,   flaunting his triumph:
"The day has dawned,   you've lost your dear ones;
you can blame yourself too   for what happened to your
     brothers."

Gudrun said:
"You're well content, Atli,   to tell me of the killing,
but you'll regret it   before it's over.
This is the legacy   my brothers left behind them:
nothing will go right for you   while I remain alive."

Atli said:
"I don't believe that;   I see a better way,
and pleasanter—   why not choose peace?
I will comfort you   with kingly treasures,
snow-white silver,   as much as you desire."

Gudrun said:
"Don't waste time hoping   that gifts will help you;
often in the past   I broke the peace for less.
If I seemed strong before,   now I'll be more so;
I'd have agreed to anything,   were Hogni still alive.

"We two were raised   in one hall together;
we played many games,   grew up in the woodland,

---

using his toes. Gunnar's hands were tied.

Grimhild gave us   gold and necklaces.
Nothing you can do   atones for their deaths;
there's no way at all   to make me think well of you.

"Women have to pay for   men's pride and power,
the chess king surrenders   if his warriors are captured,
if its roots are stricken,   the tree won't stand;
now you alone   must rule here, Atli."

Atli was so gullible   that Gudrun convinced him,
although what she kept hidden   was not hard to see.
Gudrun was crafty,   her words were clever;
she said he had persuaded her,   and played a double game.

She set the ale flowing   at a feast for her brothers;
Atli did the same   in honor of his dead.

They spoke no more about it;   the mead was made ready,
with a great uproar   the guests gathered.
The hard-minded woman   took revenge on her husband,
for Budli's son   wrought bitter sorrow.

She called her little ones,   and laid them on the bed.
Although they were frightened   the fierce boys did not weep;
embracing their mother,   they asked what she wanted.

Gudrun said:
"Don't question me!   I'm going to kill you;
I've long intended   to save you from old age."

The boys answered:
"Destroy your children—   no one can deny you.
Your wrath will be relieved   if you do your worst."

"Women have to pay. . . ." Here Gudrun deliberately becomes conciliating. The
reference to chess is, however, dubious, and may be a reference to trees
similar to that of the line below.

and played a double game. Literally, "a two-shield game."

She killed her young boys   with a warrior's courage—
her act was unwomanly—   she cut their heads off.
Later Atli   sent to ask Gudrun
where his sons were playing: he saw them nowhere.

Gudrun said:
"I'll go and answer him,   I'll tell Atli—
Grimhild's daughter   won't hide her deed.
You won't rejoice, Atli,   when you understand
how you called to sorrow   when you killed my brothers.

"I've slept very seldom   since they were murdered;
now you'll have reason   to remember my promise.
Your words that morning   are still in my mind—
the sun has set now,   I've something to tell you.

"Your two sons most terribly   were taken from you:
their empty skulls, Atli,   you used as ale-cups,
the mead I brought you   was blended with their blood.

"I set your sons' hearts   on a spit and roasted them,
carried them to you,   and said they came from calves;
you alone ate them,   nothing was left over,
greedily your teeth   ground them up.

"You've found out where your sons are—   few suffer worse;
I did my part,   but I'm not proud of it."

Atli said:
"Grim and cruel   your deed was, Gudrun,
to blend my mead   with the blood of my children.
You've killed the ones   who were your closest kin;
to me you have offered   only evil."

---

her act was unwomanly. An example of Norse understatement.
"you won't rejoice, Atli." There is an unannounced change of scene here.

Gudrun said:
"If I could choose   I would kill you too!
Northing is wrong   against such a ruler;
you have committed   crimes in the past—
the world has not witnessed   any so wicked—
but now you have done   another deed,
one so loathsome   you cannot go on living."

Atli said:
"We'll burn your body   when you've been stoned to death—
that way you'll have   what you've always wanted."

Gudrun said:
"Tell yourself that   tomorrow morning!
By a fairer death   I'll find the other light."

They sat together   talking bitterly,
listening to hatred,   neither of them happy.
A Niflung's anger grew,   he dreamed great deeds;
he sent Gudrun a message   menacing Atli.

She hadn't forgotten   the fate of Hogni,
and said she asked only   to be avenged.
Atli lost his life   a short time later
to Hogni's son   and Gudrun herself.

These words said the warrior,   abruptly awakened—
he knew that such a blow   could use no bandages:
"Whose hand struck down   the son of Budli?
Tell me whose cruelty   cut off my life."

---

you cannot go on living. Literally, "You have made your own funeral."

I'll find the other light. Vigfusson associates the expression "go to the other light," meaning "to die," with a judicial oath, itself perhaps influenced by Christian imagery.

A Niflung's anger. "A Niflung," *Hniflung* in the text, is Hogni's son (stanza 89).

Gudrun said:
"Grimhild's daughter   won't hide her deed:
it's by my desire   that your days are over;
with Hogni's son   I brought you to sorrow."

Atli said:
"You rushed into battle   when it was wrong,
betrayed a friend   who thought you were faithful.

"I left my home unwillingly   to ask your hand, Gudrun;
you were praised as a widow,   but said to be too proud—
that was not slander,   as we soon found out.
With a host of warriors   we traveled to my house
everything was done   to ease our journey.

"We lacked nothing: I had noble followers,
enough cattle   for everyone to eat;
we had much wealth,   and shared it with many.

"I paid a high price for you,   and heaped up treasures,
gave you thirty thralls   and seven good bondmaids—
those were worthy gifts—   and still more silver.

"You looked on that, you told me,   as less than nothing
while I held the lands   that Budli had left me;
you made plans in secret   to win a portion.

"I would see my mother,   because of you, sit weeping;
never was I happy,   once you were my wife."

Gudrun said:
"You lie, Atli,   though it matters little;
I had small pleasure   for all your promises.

---

betrayed a friend. It seems impossible that Atli could have expected loyalty
from Gudrun; on the other hand, he had every right to feel aggrieved.
I had small pleasure. Follows Boer's interpretation.

You and your brothers   were always quarreling—
half went to Hel   from this very hall;
you hated anything   that might have helped you.

"I had two brothers—   people thought us headstrong—
we sailed away together   to follow Sigurd,
steered outward boldly,   each in his own ship,
followed fate's course   until we came east.

"We killed a king there,   and took his country,
the noblemen submitted—   they feared our strength;
we freed from outlawry   whoever we called innocent,
and set in power   people who had nothing.

"Dead was Sigurd,   and I was dispossessed,
a grief-stricken woman,   nothing but a widow;
yet brought to Atli's hall   I felt tortured alive:
a hero had held me,   hard was it to lose him.

"You came home from the Thing,   and no fame followed you,
you won no cases   for yourself or others,
always falling back   and never fighting,
you'd give up quietly. . . ."

Atli said:
"You're lying, Gudrun,   that will do little
to help either one of us,   we have both been wronged.
Grant me this now   from your kindness, Gudrun,
and for our honor: have me carried out."

Gudrun said:
"I'll buy a ship   and a stained coffin,

have me carried out. A ceremonial farewell to his house after a man dies. Atli
is asking to be buried with dignity.

wax a sheet   to use for your shroud,
do everything as if   we were dear to each other."

Dead then was Atli;   his kinsmen despaired.
Gudrun performed   all that she had promised;
the wise lady wanted   to end her life
but her days were lengthened;   she died much later.

He will rejoice   who raises such children
as Gudrun and her brothers,   the brave sons of Gjuki;
nowhere on earth   as long as men have ears,
will their fiery words   ever be forgotten.

as if we were dear to each other. The Greenland poet might have written the whole poem to bring the story to this point and then turn Gudrun and Atli astonishingly into humans.

Gudrun urges her sons to avenge their sister Swanhild, and realizing that they will be killed, recounts the sorrows of her life.

Then I heard her say   savage words,
torn from her heart   by heavy sorrow;
ruthless, bitter,   Gudrun's rage
drove her sons   to avenge her daughter.

"Why do you sit here   sleeping through your lives?
Why are you not grieved   to be so gay?
You know King Jormunrek   killed your sister,
had her young body   trampled by horses,
white and black horses,   in the broad highway,
the well-trained, grey   horses of the Goths!

"Little you command   of Gunnar's courage,
no one could call you   heroes like Hogni!
You would seek revenge   for your murdered sister
if you were born   with my brothers' spirit,
or if you had the hearts   of Hunnish kings."

Then said Hamdir,   the high-minded:
"You took no delight   in Hogni's deed
when they woke Sigurd   out of his sleep
and your bed-linen,   blue-white,
was red with your husband's blood,   blood of the slain.

"For those two brothers   you took revenge
bitterly and sadly   when you killed your sons;

Gudrun's Chain of Woes: The poem is called "Gudrun's Incitement," in reference to the first stanzas. I have given it the more appropriate title used by W. P. Ker.

Then I heard her say. "I" is apparently the poet.

killed your sister. Swanhild, whose fate Brynhild foretold in *The Short Lay of Sigurd.*

were they alive now,   we could all,
one in spirit,   avenge a sister.

"Bring us the weapons   of Hunnish war-lords,
and we'll do battle   as you desire!"

Laughing, Gudrun   looked in her rooms,
chose kingly helmets   from her chests,
brought to her sons   long byrnies.
In haste to fight,   they mounted their horses.

Then said Hamdir,   the high-minded:
"Mother, I believe   that I'll come back
from the land of the Goths   without my life;
you'll find yourself   at the funeral feast
of your daughter Swanhild   and your sons."

Weeping, Gudrun,   Gjuki's daughter,
sadly went   to sit outside;
with tears on her cheeks   she began to tell
her story, woeful   in so many ways.

"I've known three halls,   I've known three hearths,
three husbands brought me   to their homes;
the first was Sigurd,   finest of all,
who was brought down   by my own brothers."

"That I supposed   the worse of sorrows,
but even greater   was my grief
when my brothers   gave me to Atli.

"The keen Huns   I called to counsel,
but I could not avenge   Atli's evil
until I struck off   the heads of my sons.

The keen Huns. The reference is not clear. It seems unlikely that Gudrun tried
to persuade Atli's own men to act against him.

"I fled to the sea,   hating my fate,
trying to defy   the Norns' decrees;
but when I would have drowned,   the high waves held me,
I came to land   and knew I must live.

"I went to bed—   what I'd hoped for was better—
a third time   with a mighty king;
I gave birth   to twin boys,
    . . .   Jonacr's sons.

"Bondwomen sat   around Swanhild,
of all my children   the one I most cherished,
my daughter Swanhild   shining in my hall,
as lovely to see   as a ray of sunlight.

"I dowered her with gold   and costly garments
before I gave her   to the Gothic king;
that was the worst   of all my woes:
he had Swanhild's   sun-bright hair
trodden in the mud   by horses' hoofs.

"But the saddest moment   was when my Sigurd,
lord of battles,   was slain in bed;
the grimmest of all,   when gleaming snakes
writhed around Gunnar   and robbed him of life;
and the keenest pain   was when they cut
the living heart   from the breast of Hogni.

"I've known so much evil. . . .

"Sigurd, bridle   the black stallion,
the fleet horse,   make haste to find me!
I cannot depend   on son's wife or daughter
who would give Gudrun   costly gifts.

to the Gothic king: Jormunrek.

I cannot depend. Gudrun's sentiments are reminiscent of Gunnar's speech in
The Short Lay of Sigurd (stanza 15), where he regrets equally the loss of Brynhild and that of her dowry. She foresees the death of her last surviving sons
and her consequent solitude.

"Remember, Sigurd,   what we used to say
when we were both   in one bed:
longing would bring you   back to me again
from Hel, as I   would come to you from Earth.

"Earls, raise up   an oakwood pyre,
let it be the highest   under heaven!
Then flames   will free the breast from woe,
heat will melt away   the heart's sorrow."

May noble warriors   and gentlewomen
rejoice in their lot   when they remember
this tale of grief   that Gudrun has told.

THE LAY OF HAMDIR

"Gudrun's Chain of Woes" repeats several stanzas of this older poem, which tells how Gudrun's last two sons die as heroes, avenging Swanhild. The age of the text very likely explains its gaps and confusions.

Sprang into sight   sorrowful deeds,
elves weeping   for their woe;
every morning   misfortune wakes,
dawn gives birth   to the griefs of men.

It was not just now   or yesterday—
much has happened   in the many years
since the time Gudrun,   Gjuki's daughter,
urged her young sons   to avenge Swanhild.

"You had a sister,   Swanhild was her name,
her husband Jormunrek   had horses trample her,
white and black horses,   in the broad highway,
the well-trained, grey   horses of the Goths.

"No proud sons   of great princes
are these last remnants   of my race.

"I am all alone   like an aspen in a forest,
bereft of kinsmen   like a fir-tree stripped of branches,
all my joy lost   like the leaves of a tree
when flames seize them   on a summer day."

Sprang into sight. . . . This stanza is probably interpolated, and certainly mysterious.

It was not just now. . . . A meaningless line has been omitted from this stanza.

white and black horses. These two lines are repeated in *Gudrun's Chain of Woes; The Lay of Hamdir* is older.

No proud sons. The meaning of this line is not certain.

When flames seize them. The "damager of twigs," translated here as "flames," has been interpreted as a cutting instrument.

Then said Hamdir,   the high-minded:
"You took no delight   in Hogni's deed
when they woke Sigurd   out of his sleep;
while you lay there in bed,   they killed him, laughing.

"Over the bed-linen,   blue-white,
so beautifully woven,   flowed your husband's blood.
Then Sigurd died;   you sat beside his body,
all your joy was gone,   by Gunnar's will.

"To make Atli suffer   you killed Erp
and murdered Eitil,   but it was worse for you;
no one should ever   lift his hand to kill
when the sword will strike   the slayer's heart."

Then said Sorli—   he had good sense:
"Why go on   exchanging useless words
with our mother—   what more is there to say?
We'll do your will, Gudrun,   and yet you'll weep.

"You wept for your brothers   and for your babies,
your closest kinsmen   killed in the feuds;
before long, Gudrun,   you'll weep for us both,
doomed, as we sit here,   to die far away."

Wild with rage,   they rode from the courtyard,
and went their way   on their Hunnish horses
over wet mountains   to avenge the murder.

Erp said   only this,
looking a hero   on his horse's back:
"Why, to a coward,   show the way—
but sometimes a bastard   can be brave."

---

as we sit here. They are sitting on their horses, ready to leave.
"Why, to a coward. . . ." This line and the following are treated as part of Erp's speech, as in Boer.

They met the clever one   as they rode along:
"Here's the brown baby   come to bring us help!"

Their half-brother said   he'd come to help his kinsmen
as fast as one foot   could follow the other.
They answered:
"What can a foot   do for its friend,
how can one hand   help another?"

Out of the sheaths   came their swords,
sharp blades,   greedy for blood;
the brothers lost   a third of their strength
by stabbing Erp;   he sank to the ground.

They shook their fur coats,   fastened on their swords,
the kinsmen of gods   dressed in costly fabrics.

They went further;   on a woeful road
they found their sister's son   strung up on a gallows,
a wind-cold wolf tree   west of the town,
guarded by loathsome beasts—   best not to linger.

Merry was the hall,   the men cheered by ale;
none of the Goths   knew enemies were coming
until they heard   a hero's trumpet.

They went to tell   the tidings to Jormunrek,
saying they had seen   helmeted Huns:

"Here's the brown baby." Erp is referred to as "brownish" for reasons unknown. His brothers must have refused to show him the way, or to allow
him to accompany them, on the grounds that he is cowardly. But Sorli's speech
in stanza 27 indicates that he, at least, knew that Erp was "a man of courage."

they shook their fur coats. Possibly magical clothing which protects them as
indicated in stanza 25.

the kinsmen of gods. This, like "god-descended" in stanza 25, is simply
flattering, not factual.

they found their sister's son. Swanhild's stepson.

"What will you do now? These warriors have come
to make you wish Swanhild were still alive."

Jormunrek laughed; he stroked his beard,
longing for battle, wild with wine,
shook his brown hair, looked at his bright shield,
and closed his fist around a golden cup:

"I'd call myself happy if I could see
Hamdir and Sorli here in my hall;
I'd bind tight bowstrings around those boys,
hang Gjuki's heirs high on the gallows."

Then said Hrodrglod of the slim fingers,
standing at the window— she spoke to the messenger:
"You have seen no serious danger—
can two men threaten a thousand Goths,
will they lay siege to a lofty fortress?"

There were sounds of tumult, ale-cups were shattered,
the hall flowed with blood from the breasts of Goths.

Then said Hamdir, the high-minded,
"You were glad, Jormunrek, when Gudrun's sons
came here to find you in your hall;
now your feet and your two hands,
mighty king, we've cast into the fire."

Then cried aloud the god-descended king,
a warrior in his byrnie, as a bear roars:
"Stone those two men! Spears will not bite,
nor iron injure Jonacr's sons."

Then said Hrodrglod. The translation of this stanza follows Boer's interpretation. Hrodrglod, looking out the window, sees the truth of the matter.

Sorli said:
"Brother, you did mischief   by opening your mouth:
words have often   led to woe.
You are brave, Hamdir,   but not very bright—
a man isn't worth much   when he's witless!

"The king's head would be off   if Erp were alive,
the great warrior   we killed on our way,
courageous as he was—   the Norns compelled me—
our own brother   whose blood we shed.

"We should not live   like savage wolves
   who slay each other,
like the Norns' dogs   devouring everything,
   wild in the woods.

"We've fought a good battle;   like eagles on a branch
we stand on dead warriors   our swords struck down.
We must die, now or later,   but our deeds have won us fame;
no man sees the night   when the Norns have spoken."

Sorli fell   in the hall's narrow end,
and Hamdir died   at the back of the house.

"Brother, you did mischief. . . ." No doubt Hamdir had shouted that they were
invulnerable to conventional weapons. The *Volsung Saga* explains that Gudrun had given them charmed armor.

"We should not live. . . ." This stanza is probably interpolated.

BALDER'S DREAMS

Odin forces a sibyl to tell him the fate of his son Balder.

At once the Aesir   went into counsel;
goddesses   and mighty gods
talking together   tried to say
why Balder was doomed   in all his dreams.

The old father,   Odin, stood up;
he saddled his horse   and rode in haste
down to the misty   lands of death
where he met   a hound of Hel.

Blood streaked its breast;   the dog bayed
as witchcraft's father   went his way.
Loud roared the Earth   where Odin rode;
to Hel's lofty hall   at last he came.

Odin rode on   to the eastern door
where a sibyl   slept in her grave.
The master of magic   chanted charms,
forced the dead witch   to rise. She said:

"Let me know   the name of the stranger
who willed me to come   this weary way.
Deep under snow   and drenched with rain,
the dew drifting over me,   I was long dead."

Odin said:
"I am calling The Wanderer,   son of War-Wise;
I'll tell you news of Earth   for tidings of Hel:
why are the benches   bright with gold,
the great hall gleaming—   who will be the guest?"

The witch said:
"The mead was brewed   to welcome Balder.
A shield lies over   the shining drink,

and mighty gods   await their grief.
You made me speak,   but you shall hear no more."

Odin said:
"Witch, I will ask   and you shall answer
until there is nothing   more to be known:
who is to be   the doom of Balder,
how is Odin's   son to be slain?"

The witch said:
"In blind Hod's hand   is the fatal branch,
high he is bearing   Balder's doom—
so will the son   of Odin be slain.
You made me speak,   but you shall hear no more."

Odin said:
"Witch, I will ask   and you shall answer
until there is nothing   more to be known:
by whose hand   is Hod to die,
who will bring Balder's   bane to the pyre?"

The witch said:
"Vali, born to Rind   in the western halls,
will one night old   avenge Odin's son.
He won't wash his hands   or comb his hair
until Balder's bane   burns on the pyre.
You made me speak,   but you shall hear no more."

Odin said:
"Witch, I will ask   and you shall answer
until there is nothing   more to be known:
who are those maidens   wildly weeping,
casting their veils   against the sky?"

the fatal branch: the mistletoe. Hod is Balder's blind brother; his act is inspired by Loki.

who are those maidens. Presumably Aegir's daughters, the waves. A subsequent question, now lost, probably revealed Odin's identity to the sibyl.

The witch said:
"You are not The Wanderer;   now I know
that you are Odin,   oldest of gods!"

Odin said:
"You are no witch,   nor are you wise,
but mother you are—   to three monsters!"

The witch said:
"Go home, Odin,   glad of your deed.
For now no man   shall meet me again
until the day Loki   leaps from his bonds,
and dark hosts ride   to the doom of the gods."

THE MILL SONG

Two giant maidens, Frodi's prisoners, grind out gold and peace in the magic mill until they finally rebel, breaking the grind-stone and prophesying destruction.

Now they have come   to the king's house,
Fenja and Menja   who see into the future;
in the hall of Frodi,   Fridleif's son,
the powerful maidens   were held as prisoners.

They were made   to work the mill,
told to keep   the grindstone turning;
Frodi permitted them   no rest or pleasure;
not for a moment   could the mill be idle.

Never silent   was the whirring song:
"Let us stop   to ease the stones!"
But he commanded them   to keep on grinding.

They sang and swung   the millstone swiftly
until Frodi's household   was fast asleep;
Menja chanted   as she milled away:

"Let's grind Frodi wealth,   let's grind him good fortune,
let's grind much treasure   on the mill of joy;
may he sit on gold,   may he sleep on down,
may he wake to happiness!   Then it is well ground.

"No one here   shall harm another,
plot any evil,   murder anyone;
no one shall kill   with a keen-edged sword
though his brother's bane   lie bound before him."

---

the whirring song: the combined song of the maidens and the mill.
Menja chanted. Except for this indication, it is not clear which of the maidens is speaking, or whether they sing in unison.

But Frodi did not answer,   except to say:
"Keep on working   as the cuckoo sings;
sleep no longer   than the stanza I recite!"

"Frodi, you are wise,   you have friends to talk with,
but you made a bad bargain   when you bought your bondmaids:
you chose them for strength   and for their looks,
but you didn't ask   about their ancestry.

"Hrungnir was strong,   so was his father,
Thjazi was even   mightier than either;
Idi and Aurnir,   those were our kinsmen,
brothers of the hill-giants,   who gave us birth.

"No mill would have come   from the stone mountain,
no heavy grindstone   hauled from the earth,
nor would a giantess   be grinding here
were it not   by our own will.

"For nine years   we did nothing but play
below the Earth   where we grew up;
we tried our muscles   at mighty feats:
we two maidens   moved the throne rock.

"When we rolled great boulders   through the giants' courtyard,
the whole world trembled   under their weight;
we hurled down   the heavy millstone,
swiftly turning,   for men to take.

"Then we two   who could see the future
went to Sweden   and found a fight;
we cut into byrnies,   broke strong shields,
clove our way   through grey-clad warriors.

as the cuckoo sings. Cuckoos apparently sing incessantly. The bird in question may, however, be a cock.

nor would a giantess. Boer says that the "giantess" is the mill itself; the passage is not clear.

"We overthrew one king,   set up another,
gave our help   to the good Gothorm;
we did not stop   until Knui was slain.

"Thus we spent   all that season,
winning fame   among great warriors;
where we struck   with our sharp spears
blood spurted,   and our blades ran red.

"Now we have come   to a king's house
to be cruelly treated,   and held as captives;
it's wet underfoot   and cold overhead
where we grind out peace   in this dreary place.

"Now we shall rest,   let the stone stand still;
I have done   my share of milling."
"I say our work   shall never stop
until Frodi agrees   that we've ground enough.

"We shall hold on   to the heavy shafts,
gory weapons—   wake up, Frodi!
Wake up, Frodi,   if you want to hear
our old songs,   our ancient lore.

"I see a fire burning   east of the fortress,
tidings of battle,   beacons blaze;
a mighty host   is marching here
to burn the castle   with the king inside.

"You will not hold   Hleidr's throne,
the red-gold hoard,   or the holy altars.
Let's pull on the handles,   sister, harder!
We're not standing warm   in the blood of the slain.

where we grind out peace. The mill literally grinds out peace, as well as gold.
gory weapons. Their song turns to war.
"I see a fire burning." The vision is prophetic, not actual.

"My father's girl   ground mightily,
seeing so many men   doomed to die;
now strong pillars   spring from the mill
bound with iron—   keep the stone turning!

"Keep the stone turning!   Yrsa's son
for Halfdane's sake   will slaughter Frodi;
people will call   Rolf Kraki
her son and brother—   that we both know."

The maidens milled   with all their might,
whirling the grindstone   in a giant-fury;
the shaft-tree shook,   the stand fell down,
the heavy millstone   snapped in two.

Then the giant maiden   spoke once more:
"We've done our work, Frodi,   and now we'll stop;
much too long   we toiled at your mill."

"My father's girl": presumably "my mother," but the giantess may be referring to herself.

much too long. This line is translated following Boer's edition.

THE WAKING OF ANGANTYR

Hervor, determined to avenge her father and his brothers, asks Angantyr for the sword Tyrfing, which lies with the Vikings in their gravemound. The sword, made by dwarfs, is infallible but accursed.

A young maiden   met a herdsman
as the sun set   on the Isle of Samsey.

The herdsman said:
"Why have you come   alone to the island?
You must find shelter   soon from the night."

Hervor said:
"I will not seek   shelter tonight;
no one I know   lives on the island.
But tell me this quickly   before you go—
where does Hjorvard   lie in his grave?"

The herdsman said:
"You are not wise   to ask the way;
traveler, you've come   to a place of terror.
As fast as our feet   can take us, let's leave!
To all who live here   loathsome is night."

Hervor said:
"I'll give you this necklace   for what I want to know—

The Waking of Angantyr: This poem is found in the *Hervarar Saga,* in which is told the story of the sword Tyrfing, stolen by King Svafrlami from the dwarfs who made it, and cursed so that it would always bring death to its bearer. Wounds made by Tyrfing never healed. The sword is won in battle by Arngrim, and then given to Angantyr, the eldest of Arngrim's twelve sons. These brothers are all killed on Samsey and buried in a single mound. Hervor is Angantyr's posthumous daughter. When she discovers who her father was she sets out to avenge him. It is for this purpose that she so desperately wants to acquire Tyrfing, and her father's reluctance to give it up is very much against the grain. The text of *The Waking of Angantyr* is that published by E. V. Gordon in his *Introduction to Old Norse* (Oxford, 1957).

you'll find it hard to frighten   a friend of warriors;
never will I take   golden trinkets,
costly rings,   to turn from my road."

The herdsman said:
"Only a fool   would linger here
to wander alone   through the shadows of night.
The fires are rising,   graves gape open,
fens and the high lands flame—   let's make haste!"

Hervor said:
"If all the island   is alight with fires,
we still need not fear   their snorting breath.
When we find   the dead warriors
we will talk to them,   not tremble!"

Swift to the forest   the herdsman fled
to hear no more   of that maiden's words,
but the staunch heart   in Hervor's breast
proved its temper   braving perils.

Now she saw the fire from the grave mounds and the living
dead standing outside. She went toward them and was not
frightened, passing through the fire as if it were smoke until
she came to the berserkers' grave. Then she said:

"Angantyr, wake!   I am Hervor,
Tofa's child,   your only daughter.
Give me from your grave   the great swift sword
that once the dwarves   forged for Svafrlami!

---

never will I take. . . . This line and the next might properly belong to the
herdsman.

the berserkers' grave. "Berserkers" is not just an equivalent for "warriors."
Angantyr and his brothers were killed when their battle madness had com-
pletely exhausted them. It is an almost supernatural state, unpredictable and
uncontrollable.

"Hervard, Hjorvard,   Hrani, Angantyr!
Wake up, all of you   underneath the tree roots,
helmed and with battle gear,   keen swift blades,
ring-mail and shields   and bright red spears.

"Much have you dwindled,   Arngrim's sons,
a mighty kindred   surrendered to dust,
when not one   of Eyfura's sons
will speak to me   on the Isle of Samsey!

"May you writhe   within your ribs,
your barrow an anthill   where you rot,
unless you let me wield   Dvalin's weapon—
why should dead hands   hold that sword?"

Then Angantyr answered:
"Hervor, my daughter,   you do wrong
to call down evils   upon us all.
You must be mad,   out of your mind,
your wits are wandering   when you wake the dead!

"No father or kinsman   built us this cairn.
Of those who stole Tyrfing,   two stayed alive;
the last warrior   won the sword."

She said:
"Let me hear the truth!   And whole in the grave
may Odin keep you   only if Tyrfing

"Much have you dwindled." Hervor reproaches the dead warriors with having
died utterly, instead of retaining the spirit which would permit them to speak.
The "living dead" mentioned in the prose above would seem to be different
from those in the mound, visible as well as audible. Or it may be that Angantyr
is the dead man referred to in stanza 17.

"No father or kinsman." Angantyr means that he was buried by his foes, which
is true; and, later in the stanza, claims that they have taken Tyrfing, which is
false.

And whole in the grave. . . . That is, may you not rot away.

is not beside you! Glad you would be
to cheat of her legacy your one child."

Then a flame rose high above the open graves. Angantyr said:

"The gate of Hel is down, graves begin to open,
flame flickers over the island;
awesome it is to look outside.
Don't stay here, maiden! Make haste to your ships!"

She said:
"Do not fight the darkness with flame—
not for all your fires will Hervor fear you!
It would take more to make my heart tremble
than the sight of a dead man standing at his door."

Then Angantyr said:
"Listen to me, Hervor, let me tell you,
daughter of princes, what will come to pass:
maiden, you will doom all your descendants;
if you trust Tyrfing, all will be destroyed.

"You will have a son, and he in time
will carry Tyrfing and trust in its might;
he will be called Heidrek, a hero,
strongest of men beneath the sky."

She said:
"Over you all I'll lay a spell
so that forever your dead flesh will lie
bound with ghosts to rot in the grave!
Now from your barrow yield me the blade
forged by dwarfs! It does no good to hide it."

He said:
"You are not at all like other people

"You are not at all like other people." This line is conjectural.

if you go   to grave-mounds at night,
helmed, in ring-mail,   spear in hand,
to stand here, warlike,   and wake us in our halls."

She said:
"Men always thought me   human enough
before I set out   to seek you here;
yield me the sword   that slices mail,
the shield-breaker,   Hjalmar's bane!"

Angantyr said:
"Under my back   lies Hjalmar's bane,
sheathed in fire,   rimmed with flame;
no woman   in all the world
would set her hands   to such a sword!"

She said:
"If you will give it up,   my hands will grasp
and keep forever   that keen sword.
I do not fear   the burning blade—
where my gaze falls,   flames bow low!"

He said:
"You are foolish, Hervor;   your brave heart
flings you, open-eyed,   to the fire;
but I will give you   the sword from the grave—
what can a man   deny a maiden!"

She said:
"You did well,   son of warriors,
when you gave me   the sword from the grave;
I would prefer   to have this prize,
prince, than to own   all of Norway."

In ring-mail. "Ring-mail" translates "metal of the Goths."
Hjalmar's bane. Hjalmar was Angantyr's bane as well.

He answered:
"You do not know—   your words betray you,
luckless woman—   what you have won!
Maiden, you will doom   all your descendants:
if you trust Tyrfing,   they will be destroyed."

She said:
"Now I will sail   across the sea
with your gift   to gladden my heart,
little caring,   son of kings,
how my children   may choose to quarrel later."

He said:
"You have the sword,   but keep it sheathed;
long may you be happy   with Hjalmar's bane!
Don't touch the blade: both edges hold
a deadly poison   worse than any plague.

"Farewell, daughter!   Gladly would I give you
the life of the twelve men   here in this mound,
all the strength   and the stubborn spirit
death has stripped   from Arngrim's sons."

She said:
"Vikings, farewell!   I'll follow my road,
and go in haste.   Be whole in your grave!
Now I have walked   between the worlds;
I have seen   the fires circling."

the life of the twelve men. It is uncertain what Angantyr means by "life" here;
it may be the life actually remaining to them, but of no use to those in the
world.
Now I have walked. Hervor probably speaks the last two lines to herself, after
she has left her father. The two worlds are life and death.

GUIDE TO PRONUNCIATION

The following guide is intended to facilitate pronunciation of proper names in the text. It includes only the main points where vowels and consonants of Old Norse differ from those of English. The distinction between long and short vowels, uncertain in the old poems, has not been indicated. Generally speaking, *a* is pronounced as in "arm," *e* as the *a* in "take," *i* as the *e* in "feet," *o* as in "note," *u* as the *ou* in "soup."

y has the sound of *ü* in the German *"Tür"* or *u* in the French *"tu,"* *ae* is pronounced as the *a* in "fate," *oe* as the *i* in "sir"; *ei* has the value of *ĕ* plus *ē*, *ey* has the value of *ĕ* plus *ü*, and *au* is pronounced as the *ow* in "now."

th, which stands for the Norse þ, is pronounced as in "tooth"; for the corresponding voiced sound, I have used *d*.

g: initially, hard as in "got"; intervocalic, when one of the vowels is an *i* or an *e*, it disappears; e.g., "Egil" (pronounced "ale") and "Aegir."

r is trilled.

In addition, it should be noted that the primary accent is always on the first syllable.

GLOSSARY OF PROPER NAMES

AEGIR. The sea god, husband of Ran. *Hymir*, 1, 3, 40; *Loki, passim.; Helgi I*, 29.

AESIR. The gods in general; in particular, that race of gods which was defeated by and combined with the Vanir. *Sibyl, passim.; High One*, 109, 143, 159, 160; *Vafthrudnir*, 38, 50; *Grimnir*, 11; *Skirnir*, 7, 17, 18; *Hymir*, 2, 3, 8, 12; *Loki, passim.; Thrym, passim.; Alvis*, 8, 10, 16, 26, 34; *Regin, passim., Sigrdrifa*, 18; *Balder*, 1.

AGNAR. Son of King Hraudung. *Grimnir*, introductory prose, 2, 3, 15.

AGNAR. Auda's brother, protected by Sigrdrifa. *Sigrdrifa*, prose following 4.

ALF. Hunding's son, killed by Helgi. *Helgi I*, 14; *Helgi II*, prose following 13.

ALF. Hrodmar's son, slayer of Helgi. *H. Hjorvard's Son*, prose following 13, prose following 34, 40.

ALFHILD. Wife of Hjorvard, mother of Hedin. *H. Hjorvard's Son*, introductory prose.

ALFRODULL. "Elf-Beam," the sun. *Vafthrudnir*, 47.

ALF THE OLD. One of Hodbrodd's warriors. *Helgi I*, 52.

ALL-FATHER Odin. *Vafthrudnir*, 53.

ALLVALDI. A giant. *Harbard*, 19.

ALOF. Daughter of Earl Franmar. *H. Hjorvard's Son, passim.*

ALSVINN. One of the horses of the sun. *Sigrdrifa*, 16.

ALVIS. A dwarf. *Alvis, passim.*

ANDVARI. A dwarf. *Regin*, introductory prose, 2, 3, 4, prose following 4, prose following 5.

ANGANTYR. A Viking, Hervor's father; buried with his eleven brothers on Samsey. *Angantyr, passim.*

ARNGRIM. Angantyr's father, slayer of Svafrlami. *Angantyr*, 11, 30.

ARVAKR. One of the horses of the sun. *Sigrdrifa*, 16.

ASGARD. The home of the gods. *Sibyl*, 16, 34; *Hymir*, 7; *Thrym*, 10, 18.

ALSVID. The "All-Wise," presumably a giant. *High One*, 143.

ATLI. Hring's son, one of Hodbrodd's warriors. *Helgi I*, 52.

ATLI. The son of Earl Idmund. *H. Hjorvard's Son, passim; Sigrdrifa*, 11.

ATLI. The ruler of the Huns; the historical Attila. *Gudrun I*, 25; *Short Lay of S., passim.; Brynhild*, 6; *Gudrun II*, 26, 30, 31, 34, 36, 37; *Gudrun III*, introductory prose, 1, 2; *Oddrun, passim.; Atli I*, passim; *Atli II*, passim.; *Gudrun IV*, 11, 12; *Hamdir*, 8 .

AUDA. Brother of Agnar. *Sigrdrifa,* prose following 4; *Brynhild,* 8.

AURGELMIR. A giant. *Vafthrudnir,* 29, 30, 33.

AURNIR. A giant. *Mill Song,* 9.

BALDER. The son of Odin and Frigg. *Sibyl,* 23, 24, 25, 53; *Vafthrudnir,* 54; *Skirnir,* 21; *Loki,* 27, 28; *Balder, passim.*

BEITI. Atli's bailiff. *Atli II,* 62.

BELI. A giant. *Sibyl,* 44.

BERA. Kostbera, Hogni's wife. *Atli II,* 35, 54.

BERGELMIR. A giant. *Vafthrudnir,* 29, 35.

BESTLA. Daughter of Bolthorn. *High One,* 140.

BEYLA. Frey's servant. *Loki,* introductory prose, 55, 56.

BIKKI. A member of Jormunrek's court. *Short Lay of S.,* 64.

BILLING. The father of a maiden loved by Odin. *High One,* 97.

BLIND. Servant of King Hunding. *Helgi II,* 2.

BODVILD. Nidud's daughter. *Volund, passim.*

BOLTHORN. A giant. *High One,* 140.

BORGHILD. Sigmund's wife, Helgi's mother. *Helgi I,* 1; *Helgi II,* introductory prose.

BORGNY. King Heidrek's daughter. *Oddrun,* introductory prose, 2, 4, 5, 6, 7, 11.

BRAGI. The god of poetry. *Loki,* introductory prose, 8, 11, 18; *Helgi II,* 20, prose; *Sigrdrifa,* 16.

BRAGI. A warrior. *Helgi II,* prose following 24.

BRASH. Byggvir, Frey's servant. *Loki,* 45.

BRYNHILD. Atli's sister, wooed by Sigurd for Gunnar. *Gripir, passim; Sigurd,* 3, 7; *Sigrdrifa,* 9, 14; *Gudrun,* 22, 23, 25, 27; *Short Lay of S., passim; Brynhild, passim.; Gudrun II,* 27; *Oddrun,* 16, 17, 18, 19, 20, 21.

BUDLI. The father of Atli and Brynhild. *Gripir,* 27, 30; *Sigurd,* 7; *Sigrdrifa,* 14; *Gudrun,* 23, 24, 27; *Short Lay of S.,* 15, 30, 56, 70; *Brynhild,* 4; *Gudrun II,* 26, 27; *Gudrun III,* 1; *Atli I,* 14; *Atli II,* 39, 56, 77, 91, 97.

BUR. The father of those who established Midgard. *Sibyl,* 4.

BYGGVIR. Frey's servant. *Loki,* introductory prose, 43–46, 56.

BYLEIST. Loki's brother. *Sibyl,* 42.

DAG. Hogni's son; slayer of Helgi. *Helgi II,* prose following 24, prose following 29, 34.

DAIN. A dwarf. *High One,* 143.

DELLING. The father of Day. *High One,* 160; *Vafthrudnir,* 25.

DISIR. Female protective spirits. *Sigrdrifa,* 9.

DVALIN. A ruler of dwarfs. *High One*, 143; *Fafnir*, 13; *Angantyr*, 8; *Alvis*, 16.

EGGTHER. A giant. *Sibyl*, 33.

EGIL. Volund's brother. *Volund*, introductory prose, 2, 4.

EIKTHRYNIR. A stag. *Grimnir*, 10.

EITIL. Son of Atli and Gudrun. *Atli*, 38; *Hamdir*, 8.

ELDIR. Servant of the Aesir. *Loki*, introductory prose, 1, 4, 5.

ERMANARIK. *See* Jormunrek.

ERP. Son of Gudrun and Atli. *Atli*, 38; *Hamdir*, 8.

ERP. A half-brother of Hamdir and Sorli. *Hamdir*, 8, 12, 15, 27.

EYFURA. Angantyr's mother. *Angantyr*, 11.

EYLIMI. A king, father of Svava. *H. Hjorvard's Son*, prose following 10, prose following 31, 32.

EYLIMI. Gripir's father, Sigurd's grandfather. *Gripir*, introductory prose; *Regin*, 15.

EYOLF. Hunding's son, killed by Helgi. *Helgi I*, 14; *Helgi II*, prose following 13.

FAFNIR. Regin's brother, the dragon who guarded the hoard. *Gripir*, 11, 13, 15; *Regin*, prose following 9, prose following 11, 12, prose following 14; *Fafnir, passim.*; *Gudrun I*, 26; *Short Lay of S.*, 1; *Brynhild*, 10; *Oddrun*, 17.

FENG. Odin. *Regin*, 18.

FENJA. A giantess. *Mill Song*, 1.

FENRIR. The great wolf, son of Loki and the giantess Angrbotha. *Sibyl*, 31; *Vafthrudnir*, 46, 47; *Grimnir*, 8; *Hymir*, 24; *Loki*, introductory prose, 10, 38; *Helgi I*, 40.

FENSALIR. The home of Frigg. *Sibyl*, 25.

FJALAR. A cock. *Sibyl*, 41.

FJALAR. A giant. *High One*, 11; *Harbard*, 26.

FIMAFENG. Servant of the Aesir. *Loki*, introductory prose.

FJOLNIR. Odin. *Regin*, 18.

FJOLVAR. A warrior, companion of Harbard. *Harbard*, 16.

FJORGYN. Thor's mother, the Earth. *Harbard*, 56; *Loki*, 26.

FJORNIR. Servant of Gunnar. *Atli*, 10.

FJORSUNG. Meaning uncertain. *Helgi II*, 20.

FITJUNG. Name unknown; the meaning seems to be simply "a certain person." *High One*, 78.

FRANMAR. An earl in King Svafnir's court. *H. Hjorvard's Son*, introductory prose, prose following 6.

FREY. One of the Vanir, a god of fertility. *Sibyl,* 44; *Skirnir, passim.; Loki,* introductory prose, 37, 42, 43, 44.

FREYJA. The goddess of love, one of the Vanir; Frey's sister, daughter of Njord. *Sibyl,* 17, 44; *Loki,* introductory prose, 29–32; *Thrym, passim.; Oddrun,* 9.

FRIDLEIF. Father of Frodi. *Mill Song,* 1.

FRIGG. Goddess of love; Odin's wife and Balder's mother. *Sibyl,* 25; *Vafthrudnir,* 1–5; *Grimnir,* introductory prose; *Loki,* introductory prose, 26–29; *Oddrun,* 9.

FRODI. A king who owned a magic mill. *Helgi I,* 13; *Mill Song, passim.*

FULLA. One of Frigg's maids. *Grimnir,* introductory prose.

GAGNRAD. Odin; the name means "counsel for victory." *Vafthrudnir,* 8–17.

GANGLERI. Odin. *Grimnir,* 12.

GARM. The hound of Hel. *Sibyl,* 35, 40, 45, 49.

GEFJON. A goddess. *Loki,* 19–21.

GEIRMUND. A lord. *Oddrun,* 29.

GEIRROD. a king, son of King Hunding. *Grimnir,* introductory prose, 2, 14, prose following 15.

GEIRSKOGUL. A valkyrie. *Sibyl,* 22.

GEITIR. Gripir's servant. *Gripir,* introductory prose, 1–5.

GERD. A giantess loved by Frey. *Skirnir, passim.*

GJAFLAUG. Gjuki's sister. *Gudrun I,* 4.

GJALLARHORN. Heimdal's horn. *Sibyl,* 45.

GJUKI. The father of Gunnar, Hogni, and Gudrun. *Gripir,* 13, 14, 31, 43, 47, 50; *Fafnir,* 41; *Sigurd,* 5; *Sigrdrifa,* 8, 10; *Gudrun I,* 4, 12, 16, 17, 18, 20, 24; *Short Lay of S.,* 1, 2; *Brynhild,* 4, 13; *Gudrun II,* 1, 38; *Gudrun III,* 2; *Oddrun,* introductory prose, 22, 28; *Atli I,* 1, 21; *Atli II,* 1, 51, 107; *Gudrun IV,* 9; *Hamdir,* 2, 21.

GLAUM. Atli's horse. *Atli,* 29.

GLAUMVOR. Gunnar's wife. *Atli II,* 6, 21, 22–28, 33.

GONDUL. A valkyrie. *Sibyl,* 22.

GOTHORM. A warrior. *Mill Song,* 14.

GRAM. "King" or "Warrior"; the name of Sigurd's sword. *Regin,* prose following 14; *Fafnir,* 25; *Sigrdrifa,* introductory prose; *Short Lay of S.,* 22.

GRANI. Sigurd's horse. *Volund,* 14; *Helgi I,* 42; *Gripir,* 5, 13; *Regin,* introductory prose; *Fafnir,* prose following 44; *Sigrdrifa,* 17, 22; *Short Lay of S.,* 36; *Brynhild,* 11; *Gudrun II,* 4, 5.

GRANMAR. Hodbrodd's father. *Helgi I*, 18, 46; *Helgi II*, prose following 13, prose following 18, 24, 25.

GRIM. Odin. *Grimnir*, 12.

GRIMHILD. Gjuki's wife. *Gripir*, 33, 35, 51; *Gudrun II*, 17, 18, 21, 24, 29, 32; *Oddrun*, 15; *Atli II*, 73, 81, 92.

GRIMNIR. Odin. *Grimnir, passim.*

GRIPIR. Sigurd's uncle. *Gripir, passim.*

GUDMUND. One of Granmar's sons. *Helgi I*, 32, 36, 40, 44; *Helgi II*, prose following 13, prose following 18, 21, 22, prose following 24.

GUDRUN. Gjuki's daughter, Sigurd's wife. *Gripir*, 33, 34, 45, 51; *Sugurd*, 3, 5; *Sigrdrifa*, 10; *Gudrun I, passim.; Short Lay of S., passim.; Brynhild*, 13; *Gudrun II, passim; Gudrun III, passim.; Oddrun*, 27; *Atli I, passim., Atli II, passim.; Gudrun IV*, 1, 7, 9, 18, 21; *Hamdir*, 2, 9, 10.

GULLNIR. Elsewhere unknown. *Helgi*, 43.

GULLROND. Gjuki's daughter. *Gudrun I*, 12, 17, 24.

GULLVEIG. A sibyl. *Sibyl*, 21.

GUNGNIR. Odin's spear, made by dwarfs. *Sigrdrifa*, 17.

GUNN. A valkyrie. *Sibyl*, 22; *Helgi II*, 7.

GUNNAR. Gjuki's son. *Gripir, passim.; Sigrdrifa*, 10, 12, 16, 17, 21; *Short Lay of S., passim.; Gudrun II*, 7, 18, 31; *Gudrun III*, 7; *Oddrun*, introductory prose, 12, 20, 21, 28, 29, 32; *Atli I passim.; Atli II*, 6, 7, 21, 25–29, 33, 60, 67; *Gudrun IV*, 3, 17; *Hamdir*, 7.

GUNNLOD. A giantess, Suttung's daughter, who guarded the mead of poetry. *High One*, 13, 105, 108, 110.

GUST. One of the early owners of Fafnir's hoard. *Regin*, 5.

GUTHORM. One of Gjuki's sons, and Gunnar's stepbrother. *Gripir*, 50; *Sigurd*, 4; *Short Lay of S.*, 20–22; *Gudrun II*, 7.

GYMIR. A giant, Gerd's father. *Skirnir*, 6, prose following 10, 11, 12, 14, 22, 24.

GYMIR. A giant. *Loki*, introductory prose, 42.

HAEMING. A son of King Hunding. *Helgi II*, introductory prose, 1.

HAGAL. Helgi's foster-father. *Helgi II*, introductory prose, prose following 1, 2, prose following 3.

HAKON. A king of Denmark. *Gudrun I*, prose following 27; *Gudrun II*, 14.

HALF. A king of Denmark. *Gudrun II*, 13.

HALFDANE. Kara's father. *Helgi II*, prose following 51.

HALFDANE. Frodi's brother. *Mill Song*, 22.

HAMAL. Hagal's son. *Helgi II*, 1, 6.

HAMDIR. Gudrun's son. *Gudrun IV*, 4, 8; *Hamdir*, 6, 21, 24, 26, 30.

HAR. The High One, Odin. *Sibyl*, 13; *Grimnir*, 12.

HARBARD. Odin. *Harbard, passim.*

HATI. A giant. *H. Hjorvard's Son,* prose following 12, 13, 18, 25.

HAVARD. Hunding's son, killed by Helgi. *Helgi I*, 14.

HEDIN. One of Hjorvard's sons. *H. Hjorvard's Son,* introductory prose, 31–35, 42, 44.

HEID. A valkyrie; *see* Gullveig. *Sibyl*, 22, 30.

HEIDDRAUPNIR. Presumably Mimir. *Sigrdrifa*, 13.

HEIDREK. A king, Oddrun's father. *Oddrun*, 1, 4.

HEIDREK. Hervor's future son. *Angantyr*, 19.

HEIDRUN. A goat. *Grimnir*, 9.

HEIMDAL. The "radiant god," the gods' watchman. *Sibyl*, 1, 19, 37; *Skirnir*, 28; *Loki*, 47–48; *Thrym*, 15, 18.

HEIMIR. Brynhild's foster-father. *Gripir*, 19, 27, 28, 29, 31.

HEL. The Scandinavian Hades; also, Loki's daughter, who rules over it. *Sibyl*, 34, 43; *Skirnir*, 27, 35; *Harbard*, 27; *Loki*, 63; *Alvis*, 14, 18, 20, 26, 28, 32, 34; *Regin*, 1; *Fafnir*, 10, 34, 39; *Short Lay of S.*, 45, 52, 65, 69; *Brynhild*, introductory prose, 8; *Atli II*, 42, 44, 52, 56, 57, 99; *Gudrun IV*, 19; *Balder*, 2, 3, 6; *Angantyr*, 16.

HELBLINDI. Odin. *Grimnir*, 12.

HELGI. The son of Sigmund and Borghild. *Helgi I, passim.; Helgi II, passim.; Gripir*, 15.

HELGI. The son of Hjorvard and Sigrlinn. *H. Hjorvard's Son, passim.*

HERBORG. A queen of the Huns. *Gudrun*, 6.

HERJAN. Odin. *Grimnir*, 12.

HERKJA. Atli's mistress. *Gudrun III*, introductory prose, 2, 9, 10.

HERTEIT. Odin. *Grimnir*, 13.

HERVARD. One of Hunding's sons. *Helgi II*, prose following 13.

HERVARD. Brother of Angantyr. *Angantyr*, 10.

HERVOR. Daughter of Angantyr. *Angantyr*, 3–7, 8, 9, 13, 17, 18, 25.

HERVOR THE WISE. A valkyrie, King Hlodver's daughter, Volund's wife. *Volund*, introductory prose.

HILD. A valkyrie. *Brynhild*, 7.

HILDOLF. "Battle Wolf"; perhaps Odin. *Harbard*, 8.

HJALLI. Atli's cook. *Atli I*, 22, 23, 25; *Atli II*, 62, 64, 65.

HJALMBERI. Odin. *Grimnir*, 12.

HJALPREK. Sigurd's foster-father. *Regin*, introductory prose, prose following 15; *Fafnir*, introductory prose.

HJALM-GUNNAR. A warrior. *Sigrdrifa*, prose following 4; *Brynhild*, 8.

HJALMAR. The slayer of Angantyr. *Angantyr*, 22, 23, 29.

HJORDIS. Sigmund's second wife. *Gripir*, 3.

HJORLEIF. One of Helgi's warriors. *Helgi*, 23.

HJORVARD. Helgi's father. *H. Hjorvard's Son, passim.*

HJORVARD. Hunding's son, killed by Helgi. *Helgi I*, 14; *Helgi II*, prose following 13.

HJORVARD. Angantyr's brother. *Angantyr*, 3, 10.

HLADGUD. A valkyrie, King Hlodver's daughter. *Volund*, introductory prose.

HLEBARD. A giant. *Harbard*, 20.

HLEIDR. Ancient capital of Denmark. *Mill Song*, 20.

HLIDSCJALF. Odin's hall, possibly Valhalla (Gordon). *Grimnir*, introductory prose; *Skirnir*, introductory prose.

HLODIN. Thor's mother, Fjorgyn ; the earth. *Sibyl*, 47.

HLODVARD. A king, *H. Hjorvard's Son*, 20.

HLODVER. Father of Hladgud and Hervor the Wise. *Volund*, 10.

HLORRIDI. Thor. *Hymir*, 4, 16, 28, 30, 38; *Loki*, 54, 55; *Thrym*, 7, 8, 14, 31.

HLOTHVER. A warrior. *Gudrun II*, 25.

HNIFLUNG. Niflung. *Atli II*, 89.

HNIKAR. Odin. *Grimnir*, 13; *Regin*, 18–20.

HOD. The blind god who killed Balder. *Sibyl*, 32 61; *Balder*, 9, 10.

HODBRODD. Granmar's son. *Helgi I*, 18, 35, 48, 51, 55; *Helgi II*, prose following 13, 16, 20, 21, prose following 24, 25.

HODDMIMIR. Mimir. *Vafthrudnir*, 45.

HODDROFNIR. Presumably Mimir. *Sigrdrifa*, 13.

HOENIR. A god. *Sibyl*, 10, 54; *Regin*, introductory prose.

HOGNI. The father of Sigrun. *Helgi I*, 17, 52, 56; *Helgi II*, 4, prose following 4, 13, prose following 13, 15, 18, 24, 26, prose following 29.

HOGNI. Gunnar's brother. *Gripir*, 37, 50; *Sigurd*, 3, 6; *Short Lay of S.*, 1, 14, 17, 44, 45; *Gudrun II*, 7, 9, 10, 18, 31; *Gudrun III*, 7; *Oddrun*, 8, 28; *Atli I, passim.; Atli II, passim.; Gudrun IV*, 3, 4, 17; *Hamdir*, 6.

HRANI. A brother of Angantyr. *Angantyr*, 10.

HREIDMAR. Father of Regin and Fafnir. *Regin*, introductory prose, prose following 5, 7–9, prose following 9, 11, prose following 11.

HRIMFAXI. Frost-Mane, the horse of night. *Vafthrudnir*, 14.

HRIMGERD. A giantess. *H. Hjorvard's Son*, 13–31.

HRIMGRIMNIR. A giant. *Skirnir*, 35.

HRING, SONS OF. Hodbrodd's warriors. *Helgi I*, 52.

HRODMAR. A king, Sigrlinn's suitor. *H. Hjorvard's Son*, prose following 6, prose following 12, prose following 35.

HRODRGLOD. A lady in Jormunrek's court. *Hamdir*, 22.

HROLLAUG. A warrior. *Helgi II,* 27.

HROPT. Odin. *Loki,* 45.

HROTTI. A sword. *Fafnir,* prose following 44.

HRUNGNIR. A particularly large giant. *Harbard,* 14, 15; *Hymir,* 16; *Loki,* 61, 63; *Sigrdrifa,* 16; *Mill Song,* 9.

HRYM. A giant. *Sibyl,* 49.

HUMLUNG. King Hjorvard's son. *H. Hjorvard's Son,* introductory prose.

HUNDING. The father of Agnar and Geirrod. *Grimnir,* introductory prose.

HUNDING. A king killed by Helgi. *Helgi I,* 10, 11, 14, 53; *Helgi II,* introductory prose, prose following 13, 40.

HUNDING. A king of Hundland. *Gripir,* 6; *Regin,* 15, prose following 25.

HUNDING'S BANE. Helgi. *Helgi II,* prose following 4.

HUNDLAND. The land ruled by Hunding. *Helgi II,* introductory prose.

HUNLAND. The land ruled by Atli. *Oddrun,* 4.

HUNMARK. The land ruled by Atli. *Atli,* 13.

HYMIR. A giant. *Hymir, passim:; Loki,* 34.

HYMLING. One of Hunding's sons. *H. Hjorvard's Son,* introductory prose.

IDI. A giant. *Mill Song,* 9.

IDMUND. An earl, father of Atli. *H. Hjorvard's Son,* introductory prose, 2.

IDUN. A goddess, the wife of Bragi. *Loki,* introductory prose, 16–18.

IM. A giant. *Vafthrudnir,* 5.

IMD. Elsewhere unknown. *Helgi I,* 43.

JORD. Fjorgyn, Thor's mother. *Loki,* 58.

JONACR. Gudrun's third husband, father of Hamdir and Sorli. *Short Lay of S.,* 62, 63; *Gudrun IV,* 14; *Hamdir,* 25.

JORMUNREK. King of the Goths. *Gudrun IV,* 2, 5; *Hamdir,* 3, 19, 20, 24.

JOTUNHEIM. The realm of giants. *Sibyl,* 8, 39; *Skirnir,* introductory prose, 10, prose following 10, 40; *Harbard,* 23; *Loki,* introductory prose.

KARA. Sigrun reborn, Halfdane's daughter. *Helgi II,* prose following 51.

KJAR. A king, father of Olrun. *Volund,* introductory prose.

KNEFRODR. Atli's messenger. *Atli,* 1, 2.

KNUI. A warrior. *Mill Song,* 14.

KOSTBERA. Hogni's wife. *Atli II,* 6, 15, 16, 14–19.

KRAKI, ROLF. A king, son of Yrsa and Hogni. *Mill Song,* 22.

LAERAD. Presumably Yggdrasil. *Grimnir,* 9, 10.

LAUFEY. Loki's mother. *Loki*, 52; *Thrym*, 18, 20.

LEIPTR. A river in Hel. *Helgi II*, 31.

LIF. "Life." *Vafthrudnir*, 45.

LIFDRASIR. "Desire for Life." *Vafthrudnir*, 45.

LODDFAFNIR. The recipient of the High One's wisdom. *High One*, 112–162.

LODIN. A giant. *H. Hjorvard's Son*, 26.

LODUR. A god. *Sibyl*, 10.

LOFNHEID. One of Hreidmar's daughters. *Regin*, 10.

LOKI. One of the Aesir, but of doubtful allegiance. *Sibyl*, 26, 42, 46; *Hymir*, 38; *Loki, passim.; Thrym*, 2, 3, 5, 7–11, 18, 20; *Regin*, introductory prose, prose following 4, 6–8.

LOPT. "High in the Air"; Loki. *Loki*, 6.

LYNGHEID. Regin's sister. *Regin*, 10, prose following 11.

LYNGVI. One of Hunding's sons. *Regin*, prose following 25.

MAGNI. Thor's son. *Vafthrudnir*, 51; *Harbard*, 9, 53.

MEILI. Thor's brother. *Harbard*, 9.

MELNIR. One of Hodbrodd's warriors. *Helgi*, 51.

MENJA. A giantess. *Mill Song*, 1, 4.

MIDGARD. The realm of men. *Sibyl*, 4; *Harbard*, 23.

MIM. See Mimir. *Sibyl*, 37.

MIMIR. The guardian of the well under a root of the Ash Tree. *Sibyl*, 20; *Sigrdrifa*, 15.

MJOLLNIR. Thor's hammer. *Vafthrudnir*, 51; *Hymir*, 37; *Loki*, 57, 59, 61, 63; *Thrym*, 2, 30, 32.

MIRKWOOD. A mysterious forest or moorland that separates the lands of Atli from those of the Gjukings. *Volund*, 1, 3; *Helgi I*, 51; *Atli*, 3, 5, 13, 43.

MODI. Thor's son. *Vafthrudnir*, 51.

MOGTHRASIR. A giant, father of maidens benevolent to mankind. *Vafthrudnir*, 49.

MUNDILFOERI. Father of the sun and the moon. *Vafthrudnir*, 23.

MUSPELL. A fire-giant. *Loki*, 42.

MYLNIR. One of Hodbrodd's warriors. *Helgi I*, 51.

NAGLFAR. The ship of the dead, made of nail-parings. *Sibyl*, 49.

NARI. Loki's son. *Loki*, 50.

NERI. A Norn. *Helgi*, 4.

NIDHOG. A serpent, or dragon, who will triumph at the Doom of the Gods. *Sibyl*, 38.

NIDUD. The king of the Njara. *Volund, passim.*

NIFLHEL. Hel, the realm of mist. *Vafthrudnir*, 43.

NIFLUNG, NIFLUNGS. Essentially, synonymous with "Gjuking." *Helgi I*, 21; *Oddrun*, 21; *Atli*, 11, 12, 17, 25, 26, 27, 53; *Atli II*, 38.

NJORD. The god of the sea. *Loki*, introductory prose; *Skirnir*, introductory prose, 38, 39, 41; *Vafthrudnir*, 38; *Loki*, 33–36; *Thrym*, 22.

NOATUN. Home of Njord. *Thrym*, 22.

NORN, NORNS. The Scandinavian Fates, who determined the world's destiny and that of each individual. As indicated in *Sibyl*, 8, they were of the race of giants. *Regin*, 2; *Sigrdrifa*, 17; *Sibyl*, 8, 11; *High One*, 111; *Grimnir*, 15; *Helgi I*, 2; *Helgi II*, 20; *Fafnir*, 11, 12, 13, 44; *Short Lay of S.*, 7; *Gudrun II*, 38; *Atli*, 16; *Gudrun IV*, 13; *Hamdir*, 27–29.

NORVI. Father of Night; a giant, son of Loki. *Vafthrudnir*, 25; *Alvis*, 29.

OD. Freyja's husband. *Sibyl*, 25.

ODDRUN. Sister, or perhaps half-sister, of Atli and Brynhild. *Oddrun, passim.*

ODIN. The father of the gods; the supreme deity. Sibyl, *passim.;* High One, *passim;* Vafthrudnir, *passim.;* Grimnir, introductory prose, 3, 4, 5, 15; *Skirnir*, 33; *Harbard*, 9, 24; *Hymir*, 2, 22, 36; *Loki*, introductory prose, 9, 10, 21–23, 58; *Thrym*, 21; *Alvis*, 6; *Helgi I*, 13, 38; *Helgi II*, prose following 29, 34, prose following 43, 50; *Regin*, introductory prose, 2, prose following 5; Fafnir, 43; Sigrdrifa, 2, prose following 4, 13, 19; *Brynhild*, 6, 8, 10; *Balder*, 2, 3, 4, 6, 8, 9, 10, 11; *Angantyr*, 15.

OKALNIR. Home of Brimir. *Sibyl*, 28.

OLRUN. A valkyrie, daughter of Kjar. *Volund*, introductory prose, 4.

ORKNING. Kostbera's brother. *Atli II*, 30, 31.

ORR. One of Hodbrodd's warriors. *Helgi I*, 49.

OTTER. Regin's brother. *Regin*, introductory prose.

RAEVIL. A sea-king. *Regin*, 16.

RAINBOW BRIDGE. The bridge between Midgard and Asgard, earth and heaven. *Helgi II*, 50; *Fafnir*, 15.

RAN. The goddess of the sea, Aegir's wife. *Helgi I*, 30; *H. Hjorvard's Son*, 19; *Regin*, introductory prose.

REGIN. Hreidmar's son, Fafnir's brother. *Gripir*, 11; *Regin, passim.; Fafnir, passim.*

RIDIL. A sword. *Fafnir,* prose following 26.

RIND. A goddess or giantess. *Balder,* 11.

SAD. Odin. *Grimnir,* 13.

SAEMORN. A river. *H. Hjorvard's Son,* 6.

SAEREID. Hunding's mother. *H. Hjorvard's Son,* introductory prose.

SAEVARSTAD. An island. *Volund,* prose following 16, 32.

SALGOFNIR. The cock who awakens the warriors of Valhalla. *Helgi II,* 49.

SANNGETAL. Odin. *Grimnir,* 13.

SAXI. A Saxon—i.e., German—prince. *Gudrun III,* 6.

SIF. Thor's wife. *Harbard,* 48; *Hymir,* 3, 15, 35; *Loki,* introductory prose, prose following 52.

SIGAR. A warrior, Helgi's messenger. *H. Hjorvard's Son,* 37–40.

SIGAR. Hogni's brother. *Helgi II,* 4.

SIGAR. Siggeir's opponent. *Gudrun II,* 16.

SIGGEIR. Signy's husband. *Helgi I,* 41.

SIGGEIR. Sigar's opponent. *Gudrun II,* 16.

SIGMUND. The son of Volsung, father of Helgi and Sigurd. *Helgi I,* 6, 7; *Helgi II,* 12, 15, prose following 19, 50; *Gripir,* 3; *Regin,* 13, 26; *Fafnir,* 4; *Sigrdrifa,* 1; *Short Lay of S.,* 39; *Gudrun II,* 28.

SIGRDRIFA. A valkyrie; the epithet means "Giver of Victory." *Fafnir,* 44; *Sigrdrifa, passim.*

SIGRLINN. King Svafnir's daughter, mother of Helgi. *H. Hjorvard's Son,* introductory prose, 1, 5, prose following 6, 36.

SIGRUN. A valkyrie, Helgi's wife; Svava reborn. *Helgi I,* 30, 54; *Helgi II, passim.*

SIGTYR. Odin. *Atli,* 30.

SIGURD. Son of Sigmund and Hjordis. *Gripir, passim.; Regin,* prose following 12, prose following 14, prose following 15, 18, 19, prose following 25; *Fafnir, passim.; Sigrdrifa,* introductory prose, 1, prose following 4, 21; *Sigurd, passim.;* Gudrun I, *passim.; Short Lay of S., passim.; Brynhild,* introductory prose, 6, 13, 14; *Gudrun II, passim.; Oddrun,* 19, 100; *Gudrun IV,* 4, 10, 17, 18, 19; *Hamdir,* 6, 7.

SIGYN. Loki's wife. *Sibyl,* 34.

SINFJOTLI. Son of Sigmund and Signy. *Helgi I,* 8, 33, 37, 42, 45; *Helgi II,* prose following 19, 22, 23.

SINRJOD. Hymling's mother. *H. Hjorvard's Son,* introductory prose.

SKADI. Njord's wife, Thjazi's daughter. *Skirnir,* introductory prose; *Loki,* introductory prose, 49–51.

SKINFAXI. "Shining-Mane," the sun horse. *Vafthrudnir*, 12.

SKIRNIR. Frey's servant. *Skirnir, passim.*

SKOGUL. A valkyrie. *Sibyl*, 22.

SKRYMIR. A giant who once carried Thor's knapsack, to Thor's discomfort. *Loki*. 62.

SKULD. A Norn. *Sibyl*, 20.

SKULD. A valkyrie. *Sybil*, 30.

SLAGFID. Volund's brother. *Volund*, introductory prose, 4.

SLEIPNIR. Odin's horse. *Sigrdrifa*, 16.

SNAEVAR. Hogni's son. *Atli II*, 31.

SOLAR. Hogni's son. *Atli II*, 31.

SORLI. Hamdir's brother. *Hamdir*, 9, 21, 26, 30.

SPORVITNIR. One of Hodbrodd's warriors. *Helgi I*, 51.

STARKAD. One of Granmar's sons. *Helgi II*, prose following 13, 27.

SURT. Lord of the fire-giants. *Sibyl*, 43, 44; *Vafthrudnir*, 19, 50, 51.

SUTTUNG. A giant, Gunnlod's father. *High One*, 104, 109, 110; *Skirnir*, 34, *Alvis*, 34.

SVAFNIR. A king, Sigrlinn's father. *H. Hjorvard's Son*, 1, 6.

SVAFRLAMI. The king who got the sword Tyrfing from the dwarfs. *Angantyr*, 9.

SVARANG. A giant. *Harbard*, 29.

SVAVA. King Eylimi's daughter, a valkyrie, Helgi's wife. *H. Hjorvard's Son*, prose following 10, prose following 12, prose following 31, 33, 38, 39–44; *Helgi II*, prose following 4.

SVEGGJUD. A horse. *Helgi*, 47.

SVIDPUD. A horse. *Helgi*, 47.

SWANHILD. Daughter of Gudrun and Sigurd. *Short Lay of S.*, 55, 63, 64; *Gudrun IV*, 8, 15, 16; *Hamdir*, 2, 3, 19.

SWAN-WHITE. A valkyrie, wife of Slagfid. *Volund*, introductory prose, 2, 4.

THAKRAD. One of Nidud's thralls. *Volund*, 37.

THEKK. Odin. *Grimnir*, 12.

THJALFI. Thor's servant. *Harbard*, 39.

THJAZI. A giant. *Harbard*, 19; *Loki*, 50, 51; *Mill Song*, 9.

THING. A parliament or court of law. *High One*, 25, 61; *Sigrdrifa*, 12, 24; *Atli II*, 103.

THJODMAR. Father of Thjodrek. *Gudrun III*, 3.

THJODRORIR. A dwarf. *High One*, 160.

THJODREK. A king of the Goths. *Gudrun III*, introductory prose, 2, 5.

THOR. The god of thunder, son of Fjorgyn (the Earth); keeper of the hammer, Mjollnir, with which he defended men and gods against the giants. *Sibyl,* 18, 47; *Skirnir,* 33; *Harbard,* introductory prose; *Hymir, passim.; Loki,* introductory prose, 57–64; *Thrym, passim.; Alvis, passim.*

THORA. Daughter of Hakon of Denmark. *Gudrun I,* prose following 27; *Gudrun II,* 14.

THRIDI. Odin. *Grimnir,* 12.

THRUDGELMIR. A giant. *Vafthrudnir,* 29.

THRYM. A king of the giants. *Thrym, passim.*

THUND. Odin. *High One,* 145; *Grimnir,* 12.

TOFA. Hervor's mother. *Angantyr,* 9.

TYR. The son of Hymir's wife. *Hymir,* 4, 6, 8, 11, 34.

TYR. The god of war. *Loki,* introductory prose; *Sigrdrifa,* 6.

TYRFING. A magical sword, forged by dwarfs. *Angantyr,* 14, 15, 18, 19, 27.

UD. Odin. *Grimnir,* 12.

ULL. A god. *Atli,* 30.

UNN. A Nereid, daughter of the sea. *Helgi II,* 31.

URD. The general name for a Norn. *Sibyl,* 12.

VADGELMIR. A river, presumably in Hel. *Regin,* 4.

VAFTHRUDNIR. A giant; the name means "mighty in riddles." *Vafthrudnir passim.*

VALGLAUMNIR. Presumably a river which surrounds Valhalla. *Grimnir,* 6.

VALHALLA. Valhöll, the Hall of the Slain. *Sibyl,* 25; *Vafthrudnir,* 38, 41, 42, 51; *Grimnir,* 7, 8; *Helgi II,* prose following 39.

VALI. Son of Odin and Rind. *Vafthrudnir,* 51; *Balder,* 11.

VALKYRIE. The word means "chooser of the slain"; the valkyries were Odin's shield-maidens, who rode to battlefields marking those who were to die and conducting them to Valhalla. Sometimes they seem to be simply female warriors, not goddesses. *H. Hjorvard's Son,* prose following 31; *Sibyl,* 22.

VANAHEIM. Home of the Vanir. *Vafthrudnir,* 39.

VANDIL. A prince (?). *Helgi II,* 36.

VANIR. Originally fertility gods, who were at one time at war with the Aesir; they are often spoken of as having knowledge of the future.

Sibyl, 15, 16; *Vafthrudnir,* 39; *Skirnir,* 17, 18; *Thrym,* 15; *Alvis, passim.; Sigrdrifa,* 18.

VAR. A goddess who was particularly attentive to oaths and formal agreements. *Thrym,* 30.

VE. Brother of Odin. *Sibyl,* 54; *Loki,* 26.

VEOR. "Holy" or "Defender of the Home"; epithets for Thor. *Hymir,* 12, 18, 23.

VERDANDI. A Norn; the name means "becoming." *Sibyl,* 12.

VERLAND. The land of men. *Harbard,* 56.

VIDAR. One of Odin's sons. *Sibyl,* 46; *Vafthrudnir,* 51, 53; *Loki,* introductory prose, 10, 11.

VIDRIR. Odin. *Loki,* 26.

VILI. Brother of Odin. *Sibyl,* 54; *Loki,* 26.

VILMUND. Borgny's lover. *Oddrun,* introductory prose, 6.

VING-THOR. Thor. *Alvis,* 6.

VINGI. One of Atli's messengers. *Atli II,* 4, 33, 34, 40, 42.

VINGSKORNIR. Sigrdrifa's horse. *Fafnir,* 44.

VOLSUNG, VOLSUNGS. King Sigmund and his descendents. *Helgi II,* introductory prose, prose following 13, prose following 18, 21, prose following 24; *Regin,* 18; *Short Lay of S.,* 1, 2, 13.

VOLUND. A famous smith, son of a Finnish king. *Volund, passim.*

WARFATHER. Odin. *Sibyl,* 1, 20; *Grimnir,* 9, 10.

WARWIND. Helgi's horse. *Helgi II,* 37.

WAR-WISE. Odin's father. *Balder,* 6.

YGG. Odin. *Grimnir,* 15.

YGGDRASIL. The Ash Tree, the center of the universe. *Sibyl,* 11, 38.

YLFINGS. Volsungs. *Helgi II,* introductory prose, 8, 48.

YMIR. One of the oldest giants, from whose body the world was made. *Sibyl,* 3; *Vafthrudnir,* 21, 28.

YNGVI. One of Hodbrodd's warriors. *Regin,* 14; *Helgi,* 52.

YRSA. Rolf Kraki's mother and half-sister. *Mill Song,* 24.